The Business of Home Daycare

By

P.A. Williams

Illustration of Peg's Pondering by Gary Drysdale

All other Illustrations by P.A. Williams

ISBN: 0-7596-7201-6

This book is printed on acid free paper.

1stBooks – rev. 2/19/02

ACKNOWLEDGMENTS

For my two sons, Anthony and J.P. who put up with all those rotten kids!
For my wonderful husband Gary, who encouraged me to follow my dreams.

Warning – Disclaimer

This book was designed to provide information on the business of in-home daycare. It is sold with the understanding that the author and publisher are not engaged in rendering any legal, accounting or other professional services of any kind. If legal or any kind of expert assistance should be needed, you should seek the help of a competent professional.

It is not my purpose to print everything on home daycare, but to give you pointers and my personal points of view. I would encourage you to read and study all the material that is out there, so you can get a better idea of the business.

Home daycare is not a get rich quick swindle but a business that one should enjoy. I have made every effort to make this manual as complete and as accurate as possible. However, there may be mistakes, both typographical and in content. Therefore, this text should only be used as a general guide.

My purpose in writing this manual is to guide, educate and help you on the possibilities of opening your own in home daycare business. The author and publisher shall have neither liability nor responsibility to any person or entity with respect to any loss or damage caused, or alleged to be caused, directly or indirectly by the information contained within this manual.

INTRODUCTION

In 1992, I was working for the State of Michigan in the prison system. The biggest prison in the world and full of criminals, of course. I was hired as a limited term employee, after being in several different positions; and one year later, I found myself jobless. It didn't matter that I hoped for a permanent position and worked my tail off. Nothing mattered except that I was jobless, with a day's notice, two boys to care for, and everything else that goes with being single and doing it all myself.

I looked all over and found lots of minimum wage waitress, cook, and dishwashing-jobs. I had an accounting certificate, a cosmetology license and experience working in a photography studio; I had been the Deputy Warden's secretary at the prison, and an administrative assistant for Ted Nugent World Bowhunters. Let's put it this way, I had sufficient experience in many different fields. Finding a job was always easy for me, it was just the pay that was bad. Eventually I took a job waiting tables in a bar and worked my way up to bartender.

I soon realized that working six days a week and bringing home "OK" money was wearing me down and not giving me the time I needed with my boys. Being a bartender for the rest of my life was not appealing to me. I knew that I had to do something, since I wasn't getting any younger. I considered all my options and decided to call the local Department of Social Services, and inquire about in-home daycare. They were great, and I got started in about two weeks with the paper work. It didn't take long until I was interviewing my first client. The rest is history.

INDEX

    1.   Am I ready for home daycare?
    2.   Making a living.
    3.   Self-employment vs the Time clock.
    4.   Other people's kids.
    5.   Issues to consider.

    1.   Set up.
    2.   Childproofing your home.
    3.   A few things to check.

    1.   Some basics.
    2.   State Regulations.
    3.   Educational programs for the provider.
    4.   Grants for my daycare.
    5.   The tolerable age for you.
    6.   Here they come in every nook and cranny.
    7.   Putting it all together.

    1.   Why insurance.
    2.   A knowledgeable agent.
    3.   Injuries.
    4.   National Safety Kids Campaign.
    5.   Phone list.
    6.   CPR and first aid.
    7.   Fire and tornado drills.
    8.   Transportation and field trips.

1

WHY OWN A BUSINESS?

Am I Ready for Home Daycare?

A few things came to mind when I thought about opening my own business. It was not that hard to become a business-person, even if you had never worked in a business-type setting. You could have a professional attitude with this job, until you play the hokey pokey with the kids, that is.

I set my own rules and hired the people I wanted to work with. I did it all and got the benefits, too. The thought of doing it for myself was a rush, and I felt good about owning my own business.

Being your own boss and running your own business will take some time and upkeep on your part. If you are the strong type and you believe in yourself, you will succeed!

Making a Living

There are many benefits to becoming an in-home daycare provider. You get to deduct a percentage of your house from your taxes, along with some home improvements, and other items that pertain to the operating of your daycare. Just know you will be staying at home a lot and working, as this is not a job where you go outside the home.

I recommend that you take a moment and write down what your current bills are at this moment, then calculate your current income. Make sure you understand that you might take quite a cut in pay. Can you afford this? What if you don't get a lot of kids right away? Can you afford to go for maybe two months, four months or even a year or longer, with less pay?

Determine your living cost at this moment, and then calculate the expense of beginning.

Consider These

- ✓ Insurance.
- ✓ Maybe an extra phone line.
- ✓ Extra food.
- ✓ Equipment, toys, art supplies.
- ✓ Childproofing your home.

Can I Handle Other People's Children in My Home?

Well, if the truth is known. NO, not always. However, when you look at it as a business, the fact that they are going home eventually makes it easier. If you already have your own children, why add to the kid or kids you already have? Then again, sometimes it's a real blessing.

Self-Employment vs the Time Clock

In assessing my work, to be able to stay at home and take care of my sons and make a decent living for us, I felt that was the answer for me. It was for me, and it will be for those of you who dare to venture.

Am I healthy?

- ✓ Can you be depended upon every day?
- ✓ Are you ready and willing to stay home every day, and do pretty much the same thing repeatedly?
- ✓ Do you go to the doctor a lot?
- ✓ Do you get colds easily?

You have to be very dependable in this line of work. People expect you there to take care of their children as they venture off to work, school, or other. If you are not a dependable person, you will lose your bread and butter fast. People won't play games with you, and I would not blame them. You must be certain that you can be at home and the hours you will be open. If you are one who likes to run here and there a lot, I would have to say that you would probably not be the type on whom I would depend.

I didn't have much of anything when I first started. Nevertheless, I was dependable for my kids and parents.

This is what keeps your business and gets you referrals from other clients. After awhile, I developed a routine and stuck to it most of the time.

Sometimes I would make it a free-for-all day. You just let the kids play. At other times, I made it an all-day-project day. The kids loved doing something every minute, and I slept great those nights. Then on other days, I would have a movie day, especially if it was raining or very cold.

Speaking of cold, if you are the kind of person who goes to the doctor a lot, you might want to consider this. Little kids sneeze and blow snot everywhere. They are always sick, and they do pass it on. You might have to go to the doctor. If you do, whom do you get to run the daycare? Your assistant, of course; but hey you have to pay them, too. There is money coming out of your pocket twice here once to your assistant, and once to your doctor, which can be very expensive. Can you handle being a little sick and running this daycare?

Peg's Ponderings

You wake up in the morning after a rough night's sleep, because you had a fever of 102 F. You are expecting a full house today. Now, a full house could be anywhere from six to twelve children, depending on what you are licensed for. (See your state guidelines)

I will use six for this example. Here come the kids. They are peppy and ready to go full force. You have taken a fever reducer and it is not working. You feel and look like crap! As the day drags on (and sometimes they do), your fever rises to 103.6 F and you feel sick to your stomach. You have two babies that are under one year old and two three-year-olds who are very demanding. You have a four-year-old who can't stop asking you questions; the other one is two, and still in diapers. One of the three-year-olds just peed in her pants, and the other one is making fun of her. The babies just woke up from their nap, and they have decided to let you know by screaming, as babies do a lot.

The phone is ringing, dogs barking, the cat wants to rub her butt on you; there are diapers to change, kids to feed, and no one is there to help you. No, it never happened to me, but it could.

Well, what do you think now? If you are the type of person who gets sick easily, if you don't like being around children who sneeze and fling snot, reconsider this business. Because being healthy is very important in this job.

Am I Patient?

Well, let's see. Can you handle other people's children telling you, "NO, I don't have to." "You are not my boss." "I am telling my dad and he will beat you up." They stick their tongues out at you, hit you, bite you, and cry because you looked at them. Do you have the patience for these children?

Peg's Ponderings

You are having a wonderful day. You have just one daycare child, I will call her "Wild Child," who absolutely will not listen to you. You are in the middle of story time, but Wild Child is not sitting on the rug with the rest of the children. Wild Child is running in circles and singing, "Duck Duck Goose," as she slaps everyone on top of their heads.

You are trying to read the story; unfortunately, no one else can hear the story, because Wild Child is attacking them. This makes the other children act up as well. All you want to do is tell a story, but this one child is making it utterly impossible for you to do this. What are you going to do? Do you have the patience to handle this situation without blowing up? There will be many situations like this that you will be placed in. You must have the patience to handle these children.

Just to let you know, this really did happen to me, and it took some time to get this Wild Child to stop being disruptive during story time and other times, as well. The way I handled story time was, I ask little Wild Child if she would like to help me read the story to the other children. Sometimes I would let her pick out a book for me to read. Sometimes I would let her show the pictures to the other children. Alternatively, she could just sit on my lap in the rocking chair as I read to the others. This seemed to work well for me; I made her a part of the story time. Yes, I let the other children participate, as well.

Do I Love Children?

One thing I thought about when I first decided to open my business was, "Do I love children? Can I love someone else's child as much as my own?" Actually,

My thoughts were, "No, I cannot love anyone's child as much as my own. However, I *can* love them." It is not hard, if you love children in general. You will find it easy to do as I did. You think about how they look up to you for comfort and trust. I could not look them in the eye and not feel some kind of love towards them. Those smiling faces, trusting looks, and the questions they ask. Sometimes you can't help but laugh. They will touch your heart and put a tear in your eye. Then there are the times you could just pull your hair out!

In this business, I found that to love a child is easy, but to get along with the parent is a challenge. Overall, I know that I can love children and treat them very well.

Do I Enjoy Messes?

Ha, ha, do I enjoy messes? Who thought that one up? I guess I did, after the fact, I never thought about this one before I opened my business. But, oh my goodness, do I like messes?

Are you the type of person who doesn't mind your house being wiped out in about 0.02 seconds? Actually, if you control it just right, you will be good to go with those messes. Let the kids make them, and let the kids clean them. That is part of the, "mess up and clean up," theory.

I had a free play time with my daycare, which was where all the kids could play with anything in the playroom they wanted, but the rules were: one toy at a time, per child. One thing out, then, when you are done, put it up, and go onto the next thing. Let the children know that this is the way it is, or they don't play. You would not believe the results you will get. You can make pick up time fun. We made a song to sing while cleaning the toy room. We would sing it over and over until the room was cleaned. "Picking up the toys… putting them away, storing them for another day…It's pick up time…pick up time…everybody do their part… It's pick up time…pick up time."

I also had a weekly treasure box. I would keep track on an individual sheet for each child, who was good that day and who was not. If they were good, they earned a sticker for that day on their sheets. If they didn't do as told and behave, they did not get a sticker. Yes, there were many times that I would not give stickers, and you know what? The next day, it was a different story. Then, at the end of the week, if they had five stickers for each day of that week, they could get a surprise out of the treasure box. I had small inexpensive trinkets for the kids to choose from. What I would actually do is, I would place three different things in the box. There was an opening in the back of the box for the children to put their hands in. They would then reach into the box and retrieve a trinket.

Children will learn that these are good lessons, especially because some children never receive any type of discipline from mom or dad, because they are to busy with their own lives, so it's up to you to let them know what you will tolerate at your home.

Trust me, they will learn in a fast way if done with kindness and love. But be firm, and stick to your words.

How About Your Family?

This is something you have to talk over with your family. They need to be a part of this, too.

When I first started I talked to my boys and they seemed all right with the concept of turning our house into a daycare. As time went on, however, they got a little sick of the other kids at their home all the time. I think that they felt a pinch of, "My mom is giving someone else attention, and not me." Therefore, I would set aside a little special time every day for just my kids. Eventually things worked out. **That was a good thing**.

Is your family going to be supportive of you, and understanding, when you are dead tired from the other children? When you don't feel like talking, walking, watching TV or anything, and you just want to go to bed? Are they going to understand that you are tired and you can't function? Ask them. Don't leave them out of the thought process for this business you are about to begin. Remember, this is their home, and you are "their" mom they are sharing.

Also, you might want to make sure they understand that they may or may not share their bedrooms with these children. Trust me, it makes a big difference to your own children. I would highly recommend that you keep your bedrooms private. Things can be broken or misplaced, and no one will know who did it. I learned from true-life experience not to share my bedrooms.

The Responsibility of "Other People's Children"

Can you handle other people's children? This is a question you must ask yourself. Other people might not think as you do. They might have raised their children differently than you. Everyone is different, and has different thoughts and different values. You might think it's ok to burp out loud at the table and just say, "Excuse me," yet another family might think it is a big deal and that it is not acceptable.

Some children might pass gas out loud and then laugh about it. Is this ok with you? Others might stick their butt on someone else, then pass gas, and laugh aloud. Others might call it a "fart." Is this ok with you? One family might think it's ok to say, "Jackass," because it's actually an animal. While you might think of this as a swear word, and you might ground one of your children for saying it.

Everyone has different house rules and values. While yours might be firm and strong, someone else might be so laid-back you would think it's crazy. Nevertheless, Hey, that's why you have house rules, and you need to stick to them.

Being responsible for children is a big concern in today's society. It is a big responsibility to become a licensed daycare provider. Having children, driving your car to the store, walking down a street, everything you do in life is some type of a responsibility, to yourself or someone else. You will be the sole person responsible for the well-being of these children while they are in your care. It will be your fault if they fall, bump their head, break a limb, lose a toy, don't eat, pinch a finger, you name it, it's your fault. You must ensure that everything goes right at your home while they are there.

No one is ever ready for an emergency. Every incident is different. You never know what to expect, or what the outcome will be. That is why the more training you have the better prepared you will be.

Something I did that helped me in an emergency, was that I put 3x5 index cards on a ring binder, I wrote each child's name, medical information, parents' phone numbers, and a contact number on each card, and I kept them right next to every phone I had in my house. In case of an emergency, I could just run to the phone, grab the cards, and there was all the information I needed.

As for broken bones and blood spewing, I was lucky, I never had to deal with a major emergency. Nevertheless, I am glad I had the training to handle such a situation should it have arisen.

Staying Calm in an Emergency

Can you handle the sight of blood? Can you handle a bone sticking out of someone's leg or arm? What about a convulsion, or a high temperature? What plan do you have should this happen? What if the parents are not where they said they would be? What then? What will you do in any type of an emergency?

First, you must remain calm. It is not going to help the situation if you freak out. If the child who is hurt sees you freak, and he or she freaks out, then everyone freaks. That is not a good thing.

That's exactly why you should have a couple of plans ready at your fingertips. I made sure I had someone within five minutes of my home who was ready and able to come at the snap of my fingers. Believe me, that is hard to do and usually doesn't last. However, if you have an assistant who works with you, it makes this situation much easier.

Full Time or Part Time?

I worked full time I needed the money, and I wanted to go full force on my business. For the first year, I worked another job to make ends meet. I bartended on the weekends.

Yes, this was hard to do I worked from 2:00 p.m. until 11:00 p.m. Monday through Friday with the daycare. After I closed my daycare on Friday night, I had to go close the bar, until usually about 3:30 a.m. I would take over at 11:30 p.m. then do the rest. Oh, Saturday mornings, I would wake up around 9:00 a.m., take care of my kids for a few hours, and then go to work. I closed the bar at 2:30 a.m., and I never got out until before 3:30 a.m. I had to restock, clean, get the people out, cash out, lock up and then go home, only to wake up and repeat this on Sundays.

This helped through the times when I had no children in my daycare. Usually the empty time didn't last long, but one never knows what to expect. There was a two-month period where I had no children at all. I had the interviews, but the parents would find someone cheaper or barter with another daycare. I was not at a point where I could barter with parents. I did get to that point, but only after a couple years.

While I was working on the weekends and running a full time business, I found myself so tired at nights that I could hardly see straight. I will tell you, running the business and working outside the home, was tough. But, somehow, I managed to make it through the entire year. After that first year, I quit my weekend job and only did daycare. I was a single mother of two boys. I had to make this work, and I did. I wanted it I put my mind to it and said, "Hey, I can."

You have to do what is best for you and your family. If you think that working part time is good, then that's exactly what you should do. However, if you are like I was, you might really want this to be your source of income and, you might go full time and full force with the business. My friend, this is up to you.

Are You Ready?

Heck, no, you're never ready. However, live and learn as you go. Just know that every day you will learn something new and have fun doing it. Be professional, and never lose sight of your dreams.

I felt the rush of a thousand lightening bolts ran through me on my first day. I had everything planned. I was going to do this at this time, and that at that time. What a joke. My first child was a baby, and he slept the entire 4 hours I provided care for him. He slept through diaper changes; he would grunt, wiggle and squirm around, but seldom wake. Wonderful baby, no trouble at all. I think that was the easiest money I have ever earned. I watched him for four months. The older he got the more alert he became; then, believe me, he was not quiet, but he was still a great baby. I got lucky.

The second and third children I acquired were brothers. They pushed every button they could push with me. They were good boys, but they were full of energy. What one didn't think of, the other did, and they would do it.

Those boys broke toys, spit, hit, called names, and locked my son out of his own bedroom. You name it, they probably did it. After about two months, they found out that Peg was not going to take this. I took away privileges no movie time, no project, no story time, time outs and talks with Mom. I toughed it out, and finally they became good kids. Don't misunderstand me they still tested the waters from time to time. Nevertheless, they turned out to be good boys. I think they were in need of tough love.

The moral of the story is, you are never ready for the unexpected. You interview them and they seem so sweet and well behaved. Then you are alone with them, and look out. Sometimes you will think you have just entered the "Twilight Zone."

Judging Your Ability as a Provider

When I first decided to open my business, I heard a lot of people say, "Oh, that should be easy, to just baby-sit all day." Well, I challenge those people to do this for one week, and then tell me just how easy it is.

There were times when I thought I would pull out my hair, all of it. Then there were times when I thought, this is so neat, I love this job. Remember, as with any job, there will be good days and bad days.

I feel that there are many ways you can judge your ability as a provider, even as a parent. You have just read a few things I judged myself on before I started my business. You might want to consider them, as well.

2

IS MY HOME READY?

Set Up

I had a two-story townhouse when I was doing daycare. I converted the living room and the kitchen into a pre-school setting. It was complete with little chairs and tables, cubbies, chalkboard, shelves for toys. It looked just like a miniature pre-school room. My walls were white, I covered them with lots of posters and learning things. I even used alphabets with sign language for the border. I had a place to hang wet paintings. We always put up drawings that the children did. I had a TV and VCR, so that when it was time for rest, that was easy, as well. Worked great!

Child Proofing Your Home

State regulations require you to child proof to a certain extent. I feel, and I am sure a lot of providers might agree, that you need to take the extra time and do a little more child proofing than required. Remember, you can never be too safe. Homeowners often overlook small safety hazards. After I opened for business, I started noticing things around the house I would have never thought about before, so I went through my house with a fine-tooth comb.

The guide list on page 81 is to aid in the safety of proofing your home. You will need to check with your licensing bureau, as they will direct you in this area.

Peg's Ponderings

Let's say you don't child proof your home and you are doing childcare. You have no locks on your kitchen drawers, and you keep your sharp knives in one of them. Here comes little Johnny, who is two years old. Boy, is he a busy one. He gets into everything.

He gets into your kitchen drawer and decides to play with a knife, the sharpest one, and, of course the biggest one, too. Oh, boy, he turns around to show you what he has found and oops! he slips on the floor, falls on his face, the knife goes into his stomach.

You Think about this before you tell yourself, "I don't need to childproof my home. It's safe enough, and my kids never got into stuff like that." Guess what these are not your children. You need to think about their safety as well as yours, legally and morally.

Johnny's parents are certainly going to sue you! Then what? Do you become a bag lady? Harsh thoughts, huh? Well these thoughts are real, and it can happen, to anyone.

Sure, you can safety proof your home. Just follow your state guidelines and anything else you can think of to make it a safe environment for your children, as well as daycare children.

Your Home

- ✓ Home premises, structure and furnishings: clean, safe and comfortable.
- ✓ Dangerous and hazardous materials inaccessible to all children, things such as: firearms, cleaning products, medications, laundry supplies, sharp objects, and flammables.
- ✓ Steps, stairs, porches, and elevated structures are protected to prevent falls.
- ✓ Ventilation and screening are adequate.
- ✓ Water from an approved source.
- ✓ All cupboards have childproof latches.
- ✓ One flush toilet and one water basin with hot & cold running water.
- ✓ The health department should approve your sewer system.

Fire Producing Equipment

- ✓ Make sure that your furnace, fireplace, hot water heater, pipes, wood burning stoves, and all other heat or flame producing equipment is protected to prevent against burns.
- ✓ Make sure that you do not store combustibles within four feet of plants or hot water heaters.

- ✓ If you are using portable heating devices, do not use them while doing daycare.
- ✓ Make sure you have your furnace and hot water heater inspected yearly.

Smoke Detectors & Fire Extinguishers

- ✓ Make sure you have a smoke detector for each floor, as well as a fire extinguisher.
- ✓ Make sure that the smoke detectors are located between sleeping areas and rest areas of the floor they are on.
- ✓ I recommend a heat detector in the kitchen. Check your state regulations your state might require that you have one.

Your Exits

- ✓ You will need two exits, remote from each other for each floor the children are allowed to use, one leading directly outside.
- ✓ Windows can be used as your second exit.
- ✓ Make sure that you have clearly identified your exits. I would recommend that you draw a picture of the escape plan and make sure the parents, children, and your assistants know the procedures to follow. Have drills often.

Play Equipment

- ✓ Make sure you have the appropriate equipment for the age group you are caring for. You should have a wide variety.
- ✓ You should have a playpen and crib for any children who are under the age of twelve months.
- ✓ Make sure you have a working telephone.

Indoors and Outdoors space

- ✓ Inside, there should be 35 square feet per child.
- ✓ When there is only one caregiver, you should use no more than two continuous floors for the daycare children.

✓ You should have a minimum of 400 square feet for the outdoor play area.
✓ You should have your rooms noted that are to be used for daycare.

Night Time Care

✓ Caregiver should only use two floors.
✓ Caregiver should sleep on the same floor the children are on.
✓ A third level should only be used when it has two stairways to the ground level.

3

GETTING STARTED!

Some Basics

First, I would recommend that you call your local Department of Social Services and ask for advice before you start providing care and if you decide not to obtain a license. Most states have some types of requirements for licensing providers. Some providers think that obtaining a license is a waste of time, while others will swear by it. Personally, I think it's great. I enjoyed the tax breaks, educational level, and professional attitude it gave me not to mention the benefits of being my own boss.

Remember, being licensed doesn't mean you are a wonderful person or that you are the best for this position. It doesn't mean that everyone should bring his or her children to you. Being licensed means, you have registered with the state to provide care in your home. The numbers of providers who are licensed is small next to the number of non-licensed providers. However, being unlicensed means you don't get all the tax breaks and perks that you can receive, not to mention being able to purchase insurance for the business.

Being licensed is up to you, but I would highly recommend it!

State Regulations

Every state has different regulations. Some states require you to obtain a state license, while others only require you to be registered. The child ratio varies from state to state, as well. Some states will make you claim your own children while you are doing daycare others might not. Because of these differences, you need to contact your local state licensing office to obtain your state's regulations.

Educational Programs for the Provider

Your educational requirements for daycare are determined by the state in which you reside. Some state's require you to take introductory classes before you open. You can contact your local colleges, Department of Social Service and American Red Cross. Ask them if they have any classes that you might want to take. You want to take as many as possible and get all the education you can. I suggest you enroll in a class or two, or as many as you would like, and learn about your business and what you can do to better yourself and your business.

What do I mean take classes? I don't care what your age is, or how many children you have, or have taken care of in your lifetime, you need to get some new education on the subject. You would not believe how much fun it is to go to college or to take some kind of short class that may be held in your area.

17

When I first returned to college, I decided to take some psychology classes. **Then** After the first one, I took more in that field, then classes in accounting, computers, and public speaking. I kept going until I received my associate's degree, and kept going even after that. I still take classes to further my new career.

There were public classes from the different childcare agencies in my area that offered many different choices of classes. Some were six weeks long, one or two nights per week. Others were longer or shorter; it depended on the class. I received many certifications and a degree that helped me in my business as well as with my personal self-esteem. I feel you should do this because it will bring you into the eyes of the public and get you out there with others in your field. You can even join support groups those are wonderful. So do it, this is a good thing!

Grants for My Daycare

You can obtain several grants for your business. Here is a list of things I did in order to receive grants for bettering my daycare.

- ✓ Call the local Attorney General's office. Ask for the Charitable Trust Division.
- ✓ Call large business in your area. They will sometimes help if the cost is not too much, such as funding playground equipment.
- ✓ Look for foundations and corporations that support local families and children. A lot of these institutions appreciate a phone call prior to submission of a grant request.

The Tolerable Age for You

The age group you would like to work with will greatly influence the way you will set up your activities, as well as your special room (play room). First, think about the age group you would like to provide for. During my first two years in business, I took ages six weeks to fourteen years. Then I decided, after getting a lot more experience and education in the childcare and psychology field, to run a pre-school setting. I began accepting ages three years to six years only, at that point.

I enjoyed that age, for me it was wonderful. I enjoyed teaching the children ABC's and 123's. I even taught them sign language and Spanish. Don't get me wrong, I enjoyed the mix of children I had when I took all ages. But for me, the better age group was three to six year olds.

It was, enjoyable for me to work with potty trained, no bottle drinking, walking, question asking kids, rather than babies. Children over the age of six went to school most of the day, so they represented less of a sales opportunity.

With this I am saying, ask yourself what age group it is that you really enjoy working with. Then you can figure out your business situation. I will end this section by saying a lot of parents appreciate someone who specializes in certain age groups rather than someone who accepts all ages. Something to think about!

Here They Come, in Every Nook and Cranny

Ok, I am licensed. My home is childproofed and I am ready for my children. Now what?

Planning is everything. Here are some tips on how to put it all together and make it happen for yourself.

- ✓ Relax. Take a deep breath and smile.
- ✓ Make sure you go over all agreements with parents.
- ✓ Make sure everyone knows your rules and discipline policies.
- ✓ Keep smiling.
- ✓ Have your menus planned out a week in advance. It saves you time & money. (Trust me)
- ✓ Have your projects and activities planned out for the week; and a backup plan, just in case.
- ✓ Are you still smiling?
- ✓ Keep all receipts!

Everything will work for you when you are ready to open. You will do things one-way, change them, and change them again.

You will make changes until you get everything right. You might even make changes to your hair, who knows? Change is good, especially if it upgrade's your business and your success and yourself. Hang in there. This is a good thing!

Putting it All Together

Understand, there will be some stress with this business. To be successful, you must want to triumph over anything that stands in your way. Don't let others talk you out of becoming something you know you can be, and this is not the army talking.

19

Every business has its challenges. Whether from money, people, state issues or whatever, they all have them. The way you choose to deal with them is the key to your success.

Here is a list of things I wish someone had shared with me when I first started. I think it would have helped me tremendously in the beginning.

- ✓ Take control of your business right from the start.
- ✓ Keep excellent records of money spent, received and all bills paid. At first I kept my records by hand. I used a fourteen-column spreadsheet. I soon heard about these really cool things called computers, so I purchased one and used Quicken software. Record keeping became a breeze.
- ✓ Review your agreements at least every three months and make changes if necessary.
- ✓ Stick to your policies and rules. Don't bend or compromise on rules, fees or anything. Once you do, you have a flashing neon light on your forehead, which says, "SUCKER!" They will see it, trust me.
- ✓ Any problems that arise should be addressed immediately.
- ✓ There is a lot to think about your books, activities, files, daily responsibilities and much more. Putting these things in order will take major planning, knowledge, experience, and, most of all, organizational skills.

I recommend you write out a list, look at it, and revise your schedule every day until you have complete confidence in your plan and you are comfortable. Tell yourself that you are a wonderful person, you are an entrepreneur, and you will succeed.

4

PREPARE FOR THE UNEXPECTED

Why Insurance?

Childcare providers are at risk of financial loss. If you are a provider, and a child is injured while in your care, you may have to pay the victim's hospital and doctor bills. There may be a lawsuit, and damages could be awarded to the parents. Sometimes the provider even has to pay the court costs and the attorneys' fees.

Some providers feel that there is no need for them to spend money on insurance. They think, "Nothing has ever happened to me. I am a good person." If you think accidents don't happen to good people, you are living on a different planet. Wake up! If you've never had an accident, then good for you! Keep your record clean, but get insurance!

Don't think a waiver would be just as effective, because waivers "DO NOT" stand up in courts.

Liability insurance will usually pay for damages awarded by the courts and sometimes the defense costs. Medical or accidental insurance usually pays for the victim's doctor and hospital bills. Most of the liability policies will carry coverage. If your policy does not cover this, you can purchase it alone. You might check your homeowners or renters insurance and see what that policy will cover.

A Knowledgeable Agent

When interviewing an agent, make sure he or she doesn't mind if you ask a lot of questions. Listen to what they tell you. If they sound like they are in a hurry to get to lunch, go elsewhere. Your agent should want the best contract for you and your business.

Questions for Your Agent

- ✓ Does your company limit the risk, and if so, how?
- ✓ Exactly what is, and what is not, covered.
- ✓ What are the liability, accident, and medical limits for me as a provider?
- ✓ What is my deductible?
- ✓ What is the premium?
- ✓ How will I file a claim should I need to?

Injuries

Always prepare for the unexpected. Never think it happens to the other one, but not to you. Because it can happen to you. I was the other one once.

I had a full house, and everyone was outside playing. I had six children, all girls between the ages of three and six. They were playing on the swings, teeter-totter and the slide. One little girl kept going from the swing to the slide, running in front of everyone and not looking. I just knew that, while someone was swinging, she was going to be kicked in the head. I kept telling her to walk behind the swings, but she would not listen. I made her do time out, but she still kept walking in front of the swings. Finally, she jumped off the swing. As she did, her arm went up and hooked on the chain. She had dislocated her shoulder.

Her mother was not at work, where she said she would be. Dad was at a girl friend's house. They were going through a divorce. I didn't know the girl friend's phone number, but thank goodness, the older sister knew it. The girl needed treatment now. Dad came right away, and took her to the hospital. He returned her 3 hours later. Mom came late, of course (I made her pay the late fees, too). She was upset because I called Dad that was not going to look good for her at the court hearing. I asked her "Would you have rather I had left your daughter in pain?" I told her if she didn't like it, she should find care else where, because my main concern was the child. She lightened up at that point. It was a good thing, too, because I was beginning to feel as if I were on trial.

You must be prepared for anything to happen. I was almost positive that girl was going to be kicked in the head by someone on the swing set. Instead, she dislocated her shoulder. I mentally prepared myself for the kick in the head, not the shoulder injury.

I am glad my first aid was up to date and I knew what to do. (I bet this mom was glad she had a professional provider).

Peg's Injury Procedures

1.   If injury is severe, DO NOT MOVE CHILD!!
   (a) CALL 911.
   (b) Apply necessary first aid.
   (c) Cover with blanket.
   (d) Call the parent.
   (e) Have a substitute assist with the other children.

2. If injury is serious enough to require doctor's care, but not a true emergency:
   (a) Apply necessary first aid.
   (b) Call parent- who will take the child to the doctor.

Always Remain Calm

Use Helmets

If you have bikes at your daycare that you let the children ride, make sure you get some helmets for them to use.

Facts from The National Safe Kids Campaign

- ✓ Head injuries account for more than 60 percent of bicycle related deaths, more than two-thirds of bicycle- related hospital admissions, and one-third of hospital emergency visit for bike injuries.
- ✓ In 1998, nearly 362,000 children ages 14 and under were treated in the emergency room for bike-related injuries.
- ✓ Bicyclists admitted to the hospital with head injuries are 20 times more likely to die than those without.
- ✓ Bike helmets reduce the risk of brain injury by 88 percent.
- ✓ 75 percent of bike-related fatalities could be prevented with a bike helmet.

Emergency Phone List

1. First Aid:
   Number & Address
2. Emergency Medical:
   Number & Address

3. Ambulance:
   Number & Address

4. Hospital:
   Number & Address

5. Poison Control Center:
   Number & Address

6. Fire:
   Number & Address

7. Police/Sheriff:
   Number & Address

You should also have good directions and major crossroads listed at the bottom of your phone list page. It is easier to tell people how to find you in an emergency. Also helps the substitute if they need to make the call.

CPR & First Aid

Everyone should be certified! You will be more at ease when you get your certification, since you never know when you may need to use it.

I never had to use it on the daycare children. However I did use it on a baby, once.

I walked into a public restroom saw a lady standing there holding her baby. The baby was bluish and she had stopped breathing. The lady just handed her to me with tears in her eyes. A little freaked out at what I was seeing, I knew what I had to do, CPR. Swipe the mouth, turn her over pat the back, pump the chest, and give a few breaths. Then all of a sudden mucus came out, and she started breathing. Holding a blue baby that I didn't even know, then helping her to breathe, again, wow, what a feeling! I can't explain what I felt at that moment, but I was glad to see the blue fade and hear the baby cry. I looked up to see the bathroom door open and a large group of people standing there. Everyone started cheering and clapping when the baby cried out loud.

I cried. I had to take a minute for myself. You never know when you will need to use CPR. I know that I am glad I knew what to do. Parents should go through the classes. This is something that you will never forget and might never even use, but if you need it, at least you'll know it.

You can call your local American Red Cross or hospital and sign up for the classes. Just do it!

You can purchase a first aid kit at your local store or American Red Cross. I recommend that you purchase one with a mouthpiece. If you need to give mouth-to-mouth, you will be safe from vomit and communicable diseases. Being cautious and prepared is number one.

Fire and Tornado Drills

This is necessary. You should keep track of every one, and the time it takes you to do it. I never told the children when I was going to do a drill. I would just blow the whistle. The kids heard it, and they knew what to do. Every time I had a new child, within the first week I would have a fire and/or a tornado drill. Many times at the lunch table, we would all talk about what to do if a fire started or we had a tornado.

I made up a calendar just for fire and tornado drills. I would write down the day of the drill, who was here, and how long it took to get everyone out of the house and accounted for.

One extra little thing I did was, I took a large piece of cardboard and colored it red, yellow & blues, like a big flame of fire. I cut it out and put it at one of the exits sometimes when I had a drill. This let the children know they had to go to the other exit, because this one was on fire. This worked out well, because it taught the children how to use both exits, as well as both paths they should take to get to the meeting spot.

Peg's Fire and Tornado Plan

Procedures for Fire/Tornado Drills and Evacuations

- ✓ ALL PROCEDURES WILL BE EXPLAINED AT VARIOUS TIMES OF THE YEAR.
- ✓ ALL STAFF AND CHILDREN WILL PARTICIPATE IN THE DRILLS.
- ✓ DRILLS WILL NOT BE ANNOUNCED IN ADVANCE.
- ✓ HEAD COUNT WILL BE TAKEN EACH TIME.

✓ EVERYONE WILL BE IN THE DESIGNATED MEETING SPOT.
✓ NO ONE WILL RE-ENTER THE HOUSE UNTIL PEGGY GIVES THE APPROPRIATE SIGNAL.

always remain calm

Evacuation

✓ You must write a plan for the evacuation of your home in case of emergency. Post the plan and go over it with the children weekly. Make sure they know the plan and what to do.
✓ You should have a tornado, fire, and serious accident or injury plan posted in plain view.
✓ Make sure you and all of your assistants know the procedures, and what their duties are in such an event.
✓ Make sure you keep a written record of all drills. You should have at least one per month for each policy.
✓ Keep a bell, whistle or sounding horn as an alarm.

DO NOT USE THIS FOR ANY OTHER PURPOSE.

Transportation-Field Trips

✓ Make sure that, if you transport children, your vehicles are in good, safe working condition.
✓ Make sure that you use the proper devices to ensure the childrens' safety while in your vehicles such as, infant car seats and safety belts.
✓ Make sure you have written permission from each parent in order to protect yourself legally.

5

ESTABLISHING RULES, POLICIES AND AGREEMENTS

Establishing Rules

First, I examined the house rules for my own family, and then I asked myself, what can the daycare children touch and play with? What rooms can they venture into? What will I allow them to do? How do I explain this to them and make it clear?

After I thought this out, I wrote it down. I made a separate sheet for my regular house rules and one for the daycare. Stick to these rules because ever-changing rules will never work. Finally, attach the rules that you establish to your contracts.

In developing my rules I thought, how would *I* like to be treated? Being fair is very important, and consistency will get you respect from most parents.

I have found that, when the children knew the rules in my home, it helped to control their behavior. You will want to let the parents know your rules and what you will, and will not, tolerate from their children. Although there seems to be a difficult one in every crowd, just smile and be firm.

What does being fair mean to you? What is fair to a ten-year-old might not be fair to a five-year-old and so on. A good example is pick-up time. At pick-up time, everyone is supposed to pick up. Well, the three-year-old will walk around with toys in hand singing and dancing, picking up very little. As the five-year-old complains that the three-year-old is not doing his or her part to help, the eight-year-old is complaining about the five-year-old complaining. Then the ten-year-old is doing *all* the work and complaining that it's just not fair. How do you handle this one? I know most of us want to just sit back and laugh our butts off because this is actually funny. Nevertheless, to the children it could be a major catastrophe, so let's figure out what to do.

First, I have found that letting children figure most things out for themselves is best. Intervening with their small troubles could cause a much bigger problem than it's worth. In this particular case, I would hope that the toys are picked up, and when one complains to me, I'll just say, "Well, Gee-wizzer," and let it go at that. Most of the time the problem will resolve itself. However, give some thought to the different situations you may come into. There will be many, and you will want to cry, laugh, and sometimes just roll your eyes; but letting the children resolve these small things for themselves will teach them to deal with real life situations.

Here are the rules I used for my daycare. You can incorporate your home rules and daycare rules together, or on a separate sheet, as I did.

Peg's House Rules

INSIDE

- ✓ Remove your shoes and hang up your coats.
- ✓ The basement and upstairs are OFF limits!
- ✓ No back talking.
- ✓ Respect others and their property.
- ✓ Everyone will pick up after themselves.
- ✓ No bad table talk.
- ✓ Do not interrupt anyone while they are having their turn to talk.

OUTSIDE

- ✓ You are not to leave the yard.
- ✓ Put all outside toys back where you found them, when you are done playing.
- ✓ Do not pick Peggy's flowers.
- ✓ No throwing sand.
- ✓ Do not play with the water hose.
- ✓ Do not spray the cat with the hose.

More Rules Stuff

Let's talk a little about how to explain the rules of your disciplinary policy. I found that putting them on a separate sheet of paper worked best for me. In order to get it straight with the parents, you need to sit down with them and give them an initial interview. Before you have accepted their child/children. You want them to feel welcome, yet you also want them to know your policies and rules. (I will get into the interview process a little later).

I would have both policies side by side while discussing rules and discipline. I did it this way because I would explain one, point to it and then elaborate. Most parents can visualize and understand a little better if you show them as you explain things. It is kind of the "show and tell" theory. I would also add that, if you have it on paper and explain things such as policies, rules, and discipline, you are more likely to get respect from parents than someone who just says "Come on in and play!"

I always answered questions about my policies and I would ask parents if they had any questions. You will look so much more professional when you have your ducks in a row. Don't forget this is a profession, and that you are a professional.

Discipline

I know you have thought about how to discipline someone else's children. Let me tell you, it is not easy; and some parents will try to make it very tough for you. Nevertheless, remember that this is your home, your rules, and your business.

The one thing a provider will shrug about is discipline. There is no easy way to discuss discipline in your daycare home. Just be straightforward with your parents from the beginning and consistent with the children on your rules. Think it through and make a policy you can live with, and know that this should reflect your positive attitude towards childcare in general.

I tried to promote positive thinking with the children, so that they could develop a good attitude that would be positive towards life in general. Also, I try to understand each child's needs and behaviors. Every child is different, and their behavior will reflect their home rules and the teachings their parents have given them. You should try to present yourself as a role model for the children; some children don't have good role models at home. Something good will come out of showing them how to be a good person.

My motto is, if I can reach out and help at least one child, that would be great. Who knows, that just might be our next President. Reach out to these children in a positive constructive way.

This is the disciplinary policy I used in my business.

Peg's Discipline Policy

My goal is to use positive thinking with the children, to develop an attitude that is positive towards life in general. I have limits, which protect children from:

- ✓ Hurting themselves.
- ✓ Hurting others.
- ✓ Destroying (Your daycare name) materials and/or equipment.

I try to understand each child's behavior and I will attempt to handle situations, which may occur. I will always promote development. Nevertheless, I DO NOT:

- ✓ Shame them.
- ✓ Shake them.
- ✓ Confine them in a closed area.

31

✓ Spank them or deprive a child of meals, drinks, rest, or toileting.

I Do Try To

✓ Model appropriate behavior.
✓ Reinforce good positive attitudes and behaviors.
✓ Offer children different choices.
✓ Clearly outline the consequences of inappropriate behavior.
✓ Remove children from frustrating situations, which could result in a "time out."

Smoking, Alcohol and Bad Language

✓ Smoking is prohibited in daycare, and on the premises during your hours of operation. You should post a sign in clear view for all to see.
✓ The use of alcohol and bad language is inappropriate and very unprofessional while doing daycare. I would recommend that you restrain yourself from the use of either while you are in operation of your business.

Daily Activities Program

✓ You should review your daily activities with parents, along with toilet training needs.
✓ Make sure that your activities are appropriate for the ages you are caring for.
✓ I would highly recommend, that you allow parents to visit during any hours you are open, and that they be allowed to join in certain activities for special occasions.

Establishing Charges

Most providers will call around and see what others are charging before they set their own prices. I called the Department of Social Services and asked for other providers' names and numbers. This was a great idea for me, as I made a lot of new friends and found out about different clubs and organizations I could join.

I learned that pricing your rates too high will not get you clients. Pricing your rates too low will get you clients, but they might not be ones that you particularly want. I feel that it's better to have clients than not. Therefore, at the beginning of my business I set my prices in between low and high. What do I mean? Different states, towns, and rural areas rates vary. For example, I found that in Jackson, Michigan, the South side was low-for one child, 40 hours or more, the weekly cost was about $45.00 - $55.00 dollars. East side was close to that, $50.00 – 65.00. North and West sides were a little more, they were nicer areas and they charged $75.00- $85.00. That's quite a little difference, wouldn't you say?

I lived on the *West* side, and I started out charging around $68.00 a week for one child, 40 hours or more. As the years passed, and I grew and learned more about the business, I accumulated a waiting list. Therefore, I could raise my prices and ask for the highest amount, and that's just what I did. It took me about two years to get to that point. Yes, it was a struggle; and, yes, I worked my buns off; but, hey-I did it.

One thing I will mention is that when I set my prices low, I found that a lot of the parents were only concerned about what I "CHARGED" and not what could I "OFFER" them. I found that some parents were disrespectful. There were late payments, sometimes no payments, and some parents caused me grief-grief in ways of false accusations towards my daycare, me personally, and other parents and kids. Grief you don't need or care to hear about.

Nevertheless, I did get some awesome clients when I had low rates. There are many different people in this world, and every situation is different. There will always be exceptions to every rule. Everyone can have problems such as these, no matter what you charge or where you are located. In my opinion, however, you will find these problems more when charging very low rates and in not-so-great residential areas.

Here are some things you might want to consider when setting your prices:

- ✓ You should be able to operate with a decent price and make a profit.
- ✓ Babies take more time and need constant care and attention. You should charge more for them.
- ✓ Parents who have two or more children might be more apt to contract with you if, you offer a family discount.
- ✓ You should charge when clients are late; for weekend care, if you choose to do it; and dropping children off early. Charge them-this is your time, and you should not do "freebies."
- ✓ You should charge more for special services, such as special needs children. They take more time and care. You need to focus

on them as you would on a baby at times. It will depend on the special need.

Agreements

What is an agreement? It is an act of agreeing. It is a harmony of opinions. It is an agreement regarding a method of action.

Agreements don't always work, but when you have one it's much better for you business-wise and legally, if needed. You might also know that by having an agreement for your clients, this will show them that you have it together as a professional. Also, in case you had to beseech a client in court, the judge might look at you in a more professional way. Some providers will modify their agreements for some parents. I found that if you don't start making changes, you don't get burnt. I was the biggest changer of all and guess what-do you know how many times I was burnt? More than I really care to talk about.

It's your agreement, what you put in it is your business. Here is a copy of mine. I used to think it was a little harsh, until I finally stopped making changes for people. Then I would read it and explain to the clients the "do's" and "don'ts" of my business. After that things went much better.

Peg's Agreement

I/We are contracting with (your name goes here,) for childcare. The terms of the agreement is as follows.

HOURS

The program operates from (List your open – close hours and days).

FEES and OTHER CHARGES

All fees are due at the beginning of each week.

A late fee will be charged for anyone who is late. The charge begins 5 minutes after the time specified for pick-up, (my kitchen clock will calculate the time). The charge will be $1.00 per minute, per child, that you are over time to pick-up, unless other arrangements have be made and put in writing.

34

You must pay every Monday at drop-off time. Otherwise, your payment will be considered late, and a charge of $5.00 per day will accrue for each day your payment is late.

The late charges will be enforced, no exceptions!

CHECKS

I will accept your checks until one bounces, when there will be a $35.00 NSF charge, plus all bank fees. At that time I will no longer accept your checks.

RATES

2 days or less with 6 hour usage = Part Time
$18.00 per day, per child, over 1 year
$25.00 per day, per child, under 1 year
Any hours over the daily 6-hour usage will be charged $2.50 per hour, per child, plus all late fees!

3 days or more = Full Time
$85.00 per week, per child, over 1 year old
$125.00 per week, per child, under 1 year old
Should your hours go over 42 per week, the charge will be $2.75 per hour, per child.

Drop-In Service

$3.00 per hour, per child, if space is available.

FOOD

Provider will provide all food, except food for infants. Parents will be responsible for food, formula, and special dietary needs of children under the age of 1 year.

All meals will meet the guidelines of the childcare food program.

POLICIES

The proper party must give two weeks written notice for any of the following reasons:

- ✓ Vacation period for provider.
- ✓ Vacation period for child.
- ✓ Increases in childcare payments.
- ✓ Termination of childcare agreement in writing from either party.
- ✓ I will accept payments from special programs.

However, you will be responsible for the payments until they start (meaning, you pay until they do! Then you pay your pay every week).

- ✓ If you work different days and/or hours, I need your schedule for the following week by Friday at pick-up time. If you do not give me your schedule, I will assume that your hours are the same, and I will expect your child/children on the same days and times for the following week.

PICK UP TIME

Please have your child picked up and on his/her way home within 10 minutes of arrival time. I enjoy talking with all parents, but I can not give proper attention to others if you are taking up my time. If there is something you need to discuss with me, please call after my hours that day, so we can set up an appointment to talk. I really appreciate your understanding on this matter.

Toys Being Broken

If your child breaks toys and/or equipment while here at (your business name), you will be responsible for the reimbursement of that toy and/or equipment, plus the cost of my time and gas to go and retrieve another one.

Time Outs

Parents, when you arrive and your child is in time out, your child will finish his/her time out, without running to Mom or Dad. Remember-they did something wrong to get there. Time outs will be enforced and finished.

Call In's

If you are going to be late, or if you are just not coming, please call. It's only polite.

Your Children's Toys

Please, do not let your children bring their own toys here. I have toys for them to play with. However, if they need their own blanket and/or stuffed toy (baby) that's OK.

Gum and Money

Please, do not send your child with gum or money.

The gum they spit out goes on my floor and carpet, which has to be cut out and/or replaced. The coin money is played with and lost, and then a baby gets it and puts it in their mouth! This could cause a DEATH!

(Good thing I know CPR and First Aid, huh?).

ACKNOWLEDGMENTS

I acknowledge that in case of emergency, (your name) has my full permission to make temporary arraignments for my child's care. _____(Int)

I acknowledge that the rates stated here are payable in full including holidays, children's absences, and my families' vacations. _____(int.)

Holidays are as follows:

M.L.King Jr., Memorial Day, 4th of July, Labor Day, Thanksgiving Day, Christmas Eve, Christmas Day, New Year's Eve, New Year's Day. I also acknowledge that (your business name) will be closed for these days as well. _____(int)

I agree that I will pay until special programs/or other legal programs that I will accept begin to pay, I will pay stated amounts, in full, each week, as stated. I will cover any amount that any program does not cover; that will be my responsibility, and I agree to pay in full each week. _____(int)

I agree that I am buying space availability, and I agree to pay for the space on a weekly basis. I agree to pay for illness, my family's vacation time, or any other reason that I may have not to bring my child/children to (your name) for childcare.

AND: my space is for these days only: and these hours only:
_____

(int:)_____(int:)_____

I understand that in case of illness of any kind, my child will not be accepted in (your daycare name & your name.) This includes, but is not limited to: FEVERS, HEAD LICE, SCABIES, TB, and ALL OTHER TRANSFERABLE ILLNESSES. I also understand that if my child has a fever, they must be over that fever for at least 24 hours before I can return them to (Your business name/your name).

_____(INT)_____(INT)

Child's full name: _____

Parent's Signature(s): _____

_____

DL#_____

DL#_____

SS# _____-_____-_____

SS# _____-_____-_____

Place of Employment_____

Place of Employment_____

The Heat is On

Broken contracts, broke provider; you must be careful of this. Both you and the parent can break the contract; Hopefully, both parties would agree to end the services.

Sometimes, you might have a client who leaves your daycare and says nothing to you about leaving, and never coming back. That is a broken contract the parent and or parents have broken it. At this point you could try to call them, and talk to them, let them know they are still under the contract, and that, they owe you, if this be the case.

If you have in your contract; that, parents and yourself must give notice before ending it, then when a contract is ended without notice, you lose the child, money, and respect. If talking to them professionally doesn't work, than, you could go to small claims court.

Should you not address these issue's, remember, habits are easy to form and very hard to break once started. Don't let broken contracts become a habit and let it be known that you are the one providing the service to them and they need you. If this is a test, you will pass only if you stand up for yourself.

You might also want to consider bad check policies and non-payments. There might be parents who will tell you they forgot to cash their check, and can they pay you on Monday or the next time they drop off little Johnny or Susie. Don't let this become a habit. I charged an extra $5.00 dollars per day for those who *couldn't* pay on time.

Sometimes you might feel as if you're putting them down or hassling them by doing this but, hey-look at it this way, did their boss make them wait to be paid after working all week? No, I think not. So why should you be any different? Why should you have to wait just because they don't feel like paying you when you should be paid? I put this into my contract and highlighted it and made sure the parents understood what the consequences would be if the pay was late.

Teen Sitter vs. "Us"

Some parents think you should watch their children for less money. There are actually people out there that will ask you to lower your prices. They will tell you they can get the *girl* down the street for less, or their *mom* for free. Tell them to go ahead and get them. <u>DO NOT LOWER YOUR PRICES.</u> Once you start this, you will continue doing it and before long, you will lose.

I got to the point where I started telling them this: "If you want a cheap babysitter, go hire a kid. If you want a free babysitter, take them to your mom. I am a daycare provider not a babysitter and I do charge, good luck."

Then I envision what might come in to their home. This pretty girlish giggling, happy-go-lucky teen, who as soon as they walk out the door, raids their fridge, try's on clothes, mess with jewelry, uses the make up. Pretty girlish giggling, happy-go-lucky teen, might call all her friends or her boyfriend and invite him or them over. Then, They might drink beer and smoke pot. They might have sex in the bedroom and lock the children out of the room while they do this- maybe not, they might leave the door open. If not the bedroom, hey, the couch is always open. But, yea-ha, they got them for half the money, or even free. I hope they know CPR and first aid just incase. Oh, yeah-if their lucky, they might actually watch the kids. The parent's, who so badly wish to save a buck, could hire a professional, who is, licensed by the state and knows what they're doing. It's their choice."

Don't misunderstand me about teen sitters. I have hired some awesome teens to watch my kids for an evening. I trusted them fully and paid them well. I have also, hired a couple real untrustworthy teens, which did do some of the above, and it wasn't a pretty sight when momma-Peggy got home. I have this little cartoon teen-sitter vision in my head, and whenever I had a parent try to haggle price with me and say such things I would think of my, "cartoon-teen-sitter."

6

GETTING ESTABLISHED

Peg's First Interview

I remember my first interview I was so nervous, I fumbled so much. Wow! What a great learning experience. I found that the key to an easy, smooth interview is being prepared and confident.

I learned that laying out all my papers on the table, going over them, pointing at the contracts and making eye contact worked best for me. First impressions are a big thing with most people. The more confident and professional you look, the smoother the interview. That's what you want, a smooth, easy, good interview. I found that I had to sell my program, and myself to potential clients within the first five minutes of the interview.

Don't worry if not everyone signs with your program. There will be parents that just don't like you. Don't take it personally; you can have your own opinion of them, too. You don't have to sign everyone!

There are certain issues you need to discuss with clients. You should be careful about the way you express yourself, yet you need to let them know that you are running a business, that these are your rules, and you will not bend. Always allow potential clients to ask questions, and you ask questions as well. Here is a list of the things I felt were very important when I interviewed.

- ✓ My fees.
- ✓ My discipline policies.
- ✓ My applications.
- ✓ My agreements/contracts.
- ✓ The reasons that I do not accept ill children, yet still charge fees for them. I explain why.
- ✓ A quick overview of the structured layout of my daily activities and of learning materials, meals, and snacks.
- ✓ Do not hold a position for anyone! I have done this, and I have thought I would be full, and by holding a position I lost people that would probable have been great clients. Don't make this mistake!

Sometimes you are going to come across people who think of you as "just a babysitter." Yes, this is very upsetting, because you and I know that there is a lot more to running a daycare than just baby-sitting. Nevertheless, you know there are people out there who think we are lazy and unintelligent, because we have chosen this profession. Do not let those few people make you feel less than you really are. They are the ones whose first questions will be "How much?" Just let them roll off your back and don't even give them the time of day.

Remember one more thing with your interviews-you lead them. Don't let someone else lead the interview.

Peg's Ponderings

Don't let potential clients lead your interviews, and don't let them raise their voice at you. That could lead to a shouting match. That is a bad thing! Remember aggressive behavior is a shroud for a weak person. Don't be weak, take control, it's your business, your home. I always listen and repeat back to applicants, so they understand what is being said and heard. This gives them a chance to re-state things and explain as you go on with their interview. Always stay calm and cool, no matter how badly you would like to scream. Being cool, this is a good thing!

Questions Peg Would Ask

- ✓ How old are your children?
- ✓ What days and times do you need someone to care for your children?
- ✓ Are your children potty trained?
- ✓ How did you hear about me?
- ✓ How long will you need care for your child/children months, week's or days? Are you looking for someone you can stay with permanently?

Questions the Parents Should Ask:

- ✓ Are you licensed?
- ✓ How many children are you caring for at this time?
- ✓ What are the children's ages and genders?
- ✓ Do you have children? If so, what are there ages and genders?
- ✓ How much experience do you have?

✓ How long have you been licensed?
✓ Do you provide the meals and snacks? If so, what types of food do you serve?
✓ Do you allow TV and movies?
✓ What about naps?
✓ How do I pay you-weekly, bi-weekly, monthly?
✓ Do you have references, and, if so, may I call them?
✓ Do you have assistants/helpers?

When Your Telephone Rings

What do you do when the phone rings and you have inquiries about your business. Screen the calls. Listen to the way the potential client answers your questions and to the questions they ask. Sometimes this can tell you a lot about people.

✓ Match philosophies with them.
✓ Find out what services they need-baby, toddler, school aged, special needs child?
✓ Short term or long term-do they want someone for a few weeks, a month, or someone they can stay with?
✓ If you feel good about them, set up an interview.

I went on certain guidelines and tried to stick with them most of the time. Some clients have special needs that some caregivers cannot give or would rather not deal with. Certain people will spark your interest, and others will totally blow out your spark. This is where you will need to cut them short and get on with your business.

Some people will ask questions about your business and others will get personal. I feel that a question about your business is one thing, but personal matters are something else. When they get too personal, and you don't feel comfortable with the questions they are asking, let them know that you don't feel comfortable with questions that do not pertain to daycare. Keep in mind that there are a lot of child abusers out there, and these parents are thinking, hey, I need to get to know you. They can do just that, but, not in some ways.

Advertising

How did I advertise for my business? This is very easy, at least it was for me. I made flyers and took out an ad in the local newspaper. I found that my flyers did much better and were much cheaper for me to do. I bought some paper and made a flyer with little pull-off's at the bottom. I hung them at gas stations and Laundromats. I called the local factories in my area and took flyers to hang in their break rooms. I got so many phone calls and interviews I was thinking of expanding. I had to make a waiting list.

I found that people will read wall notices and peg boards more than the newspaper at least they did where I lived.

Peg's Flyer

Daycare Openings
2nd shift.
We offer many
learning activities with
a pre-school setting.
Meals & snacks.
Spots fill quickly!
Call now!
517-555-5555
ask for
Peg

Critter City USA

| Daycare Openings 555-5555 ask for Peg | Daycare Openings 517-555-5555 ask for Peg | Daycare Openings 517-555-555 ask for Peg | Daycare Openings 517-555-555 ask for Peg | Daycare Openings 517-555-555 ask for Peg | Daycare Openings 517-555-555 ask for Peg |

Figure 1.1

Questions Providers Might Ask Parents of Infants

- ✓ What do you do as a parent when your baby cries?
- ✓ How often do you feed your baby?
- ✓ How often do you change your baby's diapers?
- ✓ Do you have any other providers for this baby? If so, who are they, and when do they care for the baby?
- ✓ Do you breast feed your baby?
- ✓ How do you care for baby's formula and/or breast milk?

Infant Needs (Birth to about 16/17 Months)

Infants are dependent upon their providers. Their most important needs involve feeding, sleeping and TLC; and as much as they can get, the better off they are.

Infants develop quickly. It's important to find the best possible care for babies. As a provider, you must be willing to provide special time and care for these infants. Providers who specialize in infants are in big demand in most areas.

Questions Providers Might Ask Parents of Toddlers

- ✓ What type of discipline do you use with your toddler?
- ✓ Are you potty training yet? If so what is your method of training and discipline on this subject?
- ✓ What type of activities do you do with your toddler?
- ✓ Does your toddler still have a bottle/pacifier?
- ✓ Do you allow your toddler to play outside?

Toddler Needs (2–4 1/4 Years)

Toddlers are some of the most curious people I have ever seen. They need a safe and active environment in which to roam around and investigate. Body language and various skills are very important to a toddler's development. They need to exercise their minds and bodies a lot. As a provider, you should help their developments by offering them lots of activities-stories, music, art and many physical activities.

Questions Providers Might Ask Parents of Preschoolers

- ✓ Do you read to your child? If so, how often, and what?
- ✓ How do you discipline your child when they act up?
- ✓ Do you do any type of activities with your child? If so, what, and how often?
- ✓ What do you do when your child refuses to eat?

Preschooler Needs

These children are talkers and doers, most of them. They need to socialize with other children their own age. As a provider, you will have to help them learn that sharing is a good thing.

You will also need to teach them how to take turns with others and how to settle arguments peacefully. Preschoolers love to dress up, color and do puzzles, and they enjoy many physical activities.

Questions Providers Might Ask Parents of School-Aged Children

- ✓ What type of things do you do with your children, as in activities?
- ✓ Do you help your children with their homework? If so, how much help do you give, and do you give answers as well?
- ✓ Are your children helpful with the other children you have, or other people's children that are younger?
- ✓ Do you allow them to help you in the kitchen, garden, yard, or with other children?

Needs of School-Aged Children

School-aged children are much more independent than younger children. This does not mean that they are capable of making life decisions on their own, or of being home alone. The activities that you as the provider should employ them with should give them a challenge. You should go beyond what they learn in school. Physical activities are very important at this age, as well as at any age.

Do I Measure Up?

Have you ever felt like you just didn't measure up to someone's standards? Well, I did, until I came to the realization that I could not please everyone, so I had to please myself. Do you measure up? No, you don't. No one will ever fully measure up to another person's standards.

This is not to say that people are being judgmental, rather that everyone has different opinions on different subjects. Nevertheless, some people do judge others. But don't sweat it! If you are professional and just be yourself, you will do fine.

Actually, I found that just being myself and not doing the extra cleaning or pick up before the interview, worked well. I let my house have that good old-fashioned, lived-in look. Parents liked that a lot better than if I tried to play a different person. Remember, you are not in a drama class. This is real life.

If someone doesn't like you for yourself, then don't play with him or her. How many times have you heard your parents tell you that?

Think about what you would like to see if you were going on an interview. Would you like to see a neat, clean, perfect home? No, I would like to see someone for who they really are. I go barefoot, live in shorts, sweats, and tee shirts. I have clean floors and a neat toy room. I found that, by being me, I got a lot of word-of-mouth advertisement, since parents like it when they can actually see you for yourself.

7

RECORD KEEPING

Your Business Records

It took me time to realize how important it was to keep all of my receipts. I made very little money the first year, and I could have received a much larger refund from the government had I kept every receipt. Even if it is only fifty cents, you would be surprised how much it adds up over the course of a year.

I think I was more concerned with taking care of the kids than taking care of the books. However, I learned my lesson. This is something you must do, and do it well.

- ✓ Before you open, take a minute and organize your financial records. Figure your potential income.
- ✓ Learn to do your books correctly.
- ✓ Estimate what you think you will spend.

This is a business, and you should operate it as such. Enjoy the kids, but, hey-this is your bread and butter. Learn it, know it, and love it. This is your business and you need to be successful at it, or you will soon end up like a lot who don't realize the business end of it- "Closed, due to poor management." You must like your business, be organized, and be a manager. Success will follow.

You should keep adequate records of all your money transactions. Sometimes, as daycare providers, we think, "Well, it's only a few bucks." Or, "I will get to it later." Let me tell you, this does not work. You need to keep adequate records. Organize your books, keep ongoing records, and you will be better off in the end. I purchased a 12-pocket folder in which to hold each month's expenses. You will need a system to keep your records. Find one that works for what you need, and then just do it!

Spreadsheets

I will show you two examples of keeping track of your business. One is the old-fashioned way. There is nothing wrong with this, I did it for quite some time. This is by using a ledger sheet. I used a 12-column sheet. I recorded on the side going down the dates of what I purchased, then across the top label the columns as needed-i.e. rent, utilities, art supplies, food, insurance, cleaning supplies and so on. Each month you enter your receipts and break them down into your columns. I used a highlighter to separate the items on the receipts i.e. red for food, blue for art supplies, green for cleaning supplies, and so on. You will want to do a 12-column for each month. Keep these receipts with your column sheet.

Staple or paper clip them together and put them in a folder, so you will have them at tax time.

The second is by computer, which is awesome if you have one with a program to do financials. I used Microsoft Excel. This program was great. The spreadsheet is already there, all you have to do is type in the titles and dates. This program will also automatically add the columns as you enter your data. You can track all your spending, as well as your income from any source you may have. Once I started using this program, I learned a lot about Excel itself and about my computer. I would recommend this program for daycare as well as personal record keeping, not to mention the many more things this program can do.

The spreadsheets I show you here (fig 2.1) give you an example of how I kept my records. The set up and headings are the actual ones I used. The numbers are not true, but example's to guide you.

First sit down and-yes, you know it-get out your paper and pen. Write down all of your expenses. Everything you pay out. House payment/rent, electric, phone, food, cleaning products, auto insurance, auto repair, supplies-as in paper, crayons, etc. Write down everything you can think of. Break it into categories. You might want to contact an accountant and ask for his/her advice. They will be the one to listen to and help you figure out your spreadsheets.

If you have employees, you need to keep track of what you pay them. I kept track of what I paid my employees the same way I kept track of my monthly spending. You can use a 12-column or Excel, or a similar spreadsheet. I have also shown you a spreadsheet for a year (fig 2.2). This is how I made entries.

Fig 2.1
Peg's Monthly Spreadsheet.

MM/DD/YY	Food	Rent	Utilities	Insurance's	Cleaning	Misc.
01-03-98	$54.09		29.03			
01-05-98		515.00		263.90	3.04	
01-19-98	189.01		109.00	86.02	5.09	5.00
01-26-98	67.99		15.98		5.23	
01-29-98	204.46					4.00
Totals	515.55	515.00	$154.01	$349.92	$13.36	9.00

Fig 2.2
Peg's Yearly Spreadsheet.

MM/DD/YY	Food	Rent	Utilities	Insurance's	Cleaning	Misc.
01-98	515.55	515	154.01	349.92	13.36	9
02	495	515	154.01	86.02	24.00	13
03	525	515	154.01	86.02		28.02
04	515	515	154.01	86.02	3.68	3
05	456	515	138	86.02	3.68	
06	528	515	138		13.92	68
07	392	515	138	349.92	24.00	56
08	347	515	138	86.02		35
09	567	515	138	86.02		3
10	598	515	154.01	86.02	37.00	3.09
11	498	515	154.01	86.02	13.01	3.87
12	602	515	154.01		2.02	157.39
Totals 1998	6038.15	6180	1768.07	1388	134.67	397.39

Purchasing and Receipts

When you are just starting, ask your friends and relatives to help you out. You would be surprised at what they might be happy to get rid of, and of course you will be happy to take it off of their hands. I did that, plus I went to yard sales (GET A RECEIPT!). Second-hand stores are great place's to find bargains. I became a frequent shopper at the second-hand stores in my area. Sometimes the store employees would call me if good, sturdy toys or something I was in the market for would come in.

When you purchase things, make sure they are sturdy. Don't buy things that won't last. It will waste your money and the kids will cry when they think they broke them. I bought a lot of Fisher Price toys. They are well worth the money and out-last the kids. That's awesome!

Don't forget all those receipts I told you to keep. I used to say, "Oh, it's just a few bucks." I wish I had kept all those few bucks worth of receipts I had thrown away. I never realized how much they really do count. I am sure you will buy ice cream from the ice cream truck or pizza, stuff like that. Get a receipt! These can be used as deductions, so get them. This is a good thing.

Deductions

Track all your deductions. You should get a receipt for each one. Here is a sample list of a few things you might be able to deduct, but check with your accountant first.

- ❑ Food
- ❑ Soap
- ❑ Toilet paper
- ❑ Towels
- ❑ Tissues
- ❑ Toys
- ❑ Project supplies such as:
  - o Crayons
  - o Markers
  - o Paint
  - o Clay
- ❑ Records/CD's/tapes/movies
- ❑ Birthday and Christmas gifts
- ❑ Educational expenses
- ❑ Seminars
- ❑ Insurance
- ❑ Advertising
- ❑ Accounting/legal fees
- ❑ Auto expense-have proof of mileage, dates, and the purpose of the expense.

Some home improvements might be deductible. I believe you must own your own home (see your accountant).

Partial Deductions

Some items can be depreciated over seven years. There is a limit, however, and you need a copy of IRS code, Section 179 that allows you to do this. These are usually items that can be divided between your personal and business usage such as:

- ❑ Playpens
- ❑ Highchairs
- ❑ Car seats
- ❑ Swing sets
- ❑ Baby beds

You will need to check with your accountant for more information on this.

An Accountant

Go to your phone book and start calling. Don't' take the first one that tells you, "I've been in this business for thirty years, and I know exactly what I am doing." You need to feel comfortable with your accountant, and you want someone who works for you. A good place to start would be by asking other providers for references.

I would also suggest that you obtain the publication called "Information for Business Taxpayers," from the Internal Revenue Service. It explains how to set up your books and keep control of them. You will be allowed to claim some home improvements, food, dishes, eating utensils, blankets, pillows, toys, project items like paper, glue, crayons, markers, scissors etc. There are many things you can claim. Label your ledger and keep your receipts!

While I was doing daycare, I kept track of miles I drove my auto to and from the grocery store and other places that pertained to daycare. Keep all gas, oil, and auto repair no matter how minor they are. These are all deductible, and you will need the receipts for your taxes. You should keep them in your files for seven years.

I found that keeping very good records also reduced the cost of having my taxes done. A good accountant will appreciate you for keeping track of your accounts receivable (money owed to you) and your accounts payable (money owed by you). Trust me keeping good records benefits you in the end.

Children's Record's

You should keep the following information on each child in your care:

A) Child's full name, date of birth, dates of admission and discharge.
B) Parents' names.
C) Home and work phone numbers where the parents can be reached.
D) The home and work address of each parent.
E) Address of the family physician, clinic, and/or hospital preferred by the parent.
F) Any known allergies the child has-i.e. food, medication, mold, etc.

Make sure that you check your state's guidelines!

Your Personal Training

- ✓ Keep records of all training you take towards childcare.
- ✓ Keep your first aid & CPR certificates up to date.

Health Records

You should keep a copy of the following for each child:

- ✓ Immunization record.
- ✓ Emergency medical permission form.
- ✓ A statement claiming freedom of communicable diseases.
- ✓ Special needs statement.
- ✓ Medication records.

Medications

- ✓ Keep on file prior written permission for each child.
- ✓ Label the original container.
- ✓ Keep medications in childproof containers at all times.
- ✓ Have the instructions with the medication, in the child's file.
- ✓ Keep a copy of the child's medical records.

Communicable Disease of Yourself and Your staff

- ✓ You should have a record of medical statements and TB test results on file.
- ✓ Parents should be informed of anyone staff or children, who have not been immunized.
- ✓ You should keep your business *records (pertaining to everything)* up to date and maintained for three (3) years.

Immunization Schedule for Infants and Children

Birth to 2 weeks	HBV
2 months	DTP, Polio, Hib, HBV
4 months	DTP, Polio, Hib
6 months	DTP, Polio, HBV
6-18 months	Polio
12-15 months	MMR, Hib, V
18 months	DTP
4-6 years	DTP, Polio, MMR
14-16 years	Td

Adult Immunization Schedule

19 years +	Td	Every 10 years
	MMR	#
	HBV	#
	Polio	#
	Rubella	#
	V	#
	Influenza	Annually
55 years +	Pneumonia	Every 10 years

Keys

DTP	=	diphtheria, tetanus, pertussis (Whooping cough)
Hib	=	Haemophilus influenza type b
HBV	=	Hepatitis B virus
MMR	=	measles, mumps, rubella
Polio	=	OPV (oral polio virus) or IPV (inactive polio virus)

Please note: Check with your doctor on when each of these shots are to be administered.

Td = adult tetanus and diphtheria
(needed every 10 years throughout life)
V = varicella (chicken pox)
# = Only if there is no documentation of childhood immunizations.

The National Immunization Information Hotline can answer your questions. Call **1-800-232-2522** for more information.

8

FEEDING THE KIDS!

Child Care Food Program

What a wonderful program this is! This is one you also must be licensed or certified to receive. I would recommend that everyone join.

Congress originated this program in 1968, to develop better health of children in daycare centers. Congress hoped this program would promote better eating habits and the quality of meals. The program was expanded in 1975 to include family childcare homes. Then, in 1989, the program was re-named "Child and Adult Food Program," and adult daycares were added.

The Food and Nutrition Service, which is an agency of the United States Department of Agriculture (USDA), runs this program nationally. The program allows providers, as well as facilities, to provide healthy, nutritious meals to children. The program reimburses providers for the cost of the food that they feed the children. However, the food must comply with the programs food guidelines.

How do you get on this wonderful program? How does it work? Well, your first step is to be licensed or certified. Second, call your Department of Social Services, or use the list in the back of this book and call Child Nutritional Programs. Ask for the list of Child Care Food Programs in your area. You might want to call all the different programs in your area and find out which one best fits your needs. When you figure that out, call and tell them you are interested in joining their program. They will tell you the rest.

I can't tell you how much this program helped me over the years I was a provider. I really looked forward to the check every month.

I can recall the visits from my food program lady, Tracy. Whenever she came, all the children would yell, "Peggy, the food lady is here!" They loved Tracy's visits. She always brought puzzles and little things for the children to color. I enjoyed her visits, as well. It was always nice to talk to someone over three feet tall for even just a minute or two. She always had goodies for the children, new recipes and cookbooks for me. This program is wonderful, and the program I was in was great. Everyone was very nice and helpful to me. Go for it!

Food Requirements

Make sure the food you are serving meets each child's needs. Store all your food in proper containers and make sure they are sealed for safety and cleanliness. You might want to have a written agreement with each parent, if they are supplying the food for their child.

Inform each parent if you use homemade canned food or any other homemade foods or un-pasteurized milk products. You might even consider having them sign a statement pertaining to the use of such foods.

Peg's Menu for One Week

Breakfast

<u>MONDAY</u>

OATMEAL
APPLE
MILK

<u>TUESDAY</u>

APPLE
TOAST
MILK

<u>WEDNESDAY</u>

PANCAKE
STRAWBERRIES
MILK

<u>THURSDAY</u>

OATMEAL
BANANA
MILK

<u>FRIDAY</u>

ORANGES
TOAST
MILK

Lunches or Dinners

<u>MONDAY</u>

HAM
PINEAPPLE
GREEN BEANS

PASTA
MILK

<u>TUESDAY</u>

CHICKEN
TATER TOTS
MIXED VEGETABLES
PASTA
MILK

<u>WEDNESDAY</u>

FISH STICKS
CORN
ORANGE
ROLL
MILK

<u>THURSDAY</u>

SCRAMBLED EGGS
HASH BROWNS
ORANGE
TOAST
MILK

<u>FRIDAY</u>

HAM
CABBAGE
CARROTS
CORN BREAD
MILK

Snacks

MONDAY

1st CORN CHIPS/GRAPE JUICE
2nd ENGLISH MUFFIN/MILK
3rd COOKIE/MILK

TUESDAY

1st COOKIE/MILK
2nd GRAHAM CRACKERS/MILK
3rd CORN CHIPS/ORANGE JUICE

WEDNESDAY

1st BAGEL/MILK
2nd RITZ CRACKERS/ORANGE JUICE
3rd HOMEMADE COOKIE/MILK

THURSDAY

1st COOKIE/MILK
2nd ENGGLISH MUFFIN/MILK
3rd HAM/MILK

FRIDAY

1st GRAHAM CRACKERS/ORANGE JUICE
2nd HOMEMADE COOKIE/MILK
3rd RITZ CRACKERS/GRAPE JUICE

Snacks and Meals Favorites

Cheese Breakfast Roll-ups

Flour tortilla
¼ cup real cheddar cheese or 2 slices real cheese
Optional additions:
Eggs, sausage, potatoes (make sure these items are fully cooked before adding them into your roll-up).

Directions

Sprinkle cheese and optional ingredients on half of the tortilla. Fold the tortilla in half and microwave for about 30 – 45 seconds. Then fold tortilla into triangles, cut and serve warm.

Pancake Faces

Strawberries
Pancake mix
Bananas
Powdered sugar

Directions

Prepare pancakes as per directions on box. When pancakes are done, place a stack of two on each plate. Cut bananas in half long way to form a smile, use strawberries cut in half as eyes, use a whole berry for the nose, sprinkle sugar all over face to make a funny faced pancake.

Waffle Pizza

Frozen waffles
Peanut butter
Jelly
Banana slices

Directions

Heat waffle. Smear peanut butter, then jelly, on waffle. Top with slices of bananas.

Fruity and Veggie People Pancakes

Pancakes (cold), Peanut butter, Banana, Apples, Grapes, Raisins, Carrot strings, Celery pieces

Directions

Smear peanut butter on pancake. Slice apple in sections as half smiles. Cut bananas into small round sections as eyes. Cut grapes in half; place them on top of banana. Place raisin on grape or use them as freckles. Place carrots around the top edge for hair. Use celery pieces for arms and legs.

Peg's Conglobation

1 box Kraft Macaroni and Cheese
1 can Campbell's Mushroom Soup
1 pound hamburger
½ cup real shredded cheddar cheese

Directions

Make the Kraft Macaroni and Cheese, per directions on box. Add the ½ cup real cheese. Add ¼ *can* of water to Campbell's Mushroom Soup heat and set aside. Make meatballs with the hamburger. Mix the Campbell's Mushroom Soup with the Kraft Macaroni and Cheese, and then add the meatballs. Mix and serve. Kids love it!

Meatballs

In bowl, mix hamburger, 1 egg, about 8–10 Ritz Crackers or 1 cup Quaker Oatmeal, salt and pepper to taste. Roll into balls and cook on top of stove in small amount of water, until brown and done.

Taco Dogs

1 pack Oscar Mayer All Beef Hot Dogs
1 pack of 10-12 Old El Paso Taco Shells (hard)

Directions

Cook Oscar Mayer All Beef Hot Dogs per directions on package. Warm Old El Paso Taco Shells per directions on box. Put hot dogs in shells, add whatever you like: mustard, ketchup, chili sauce, and cheese.

9

WHY ME?

On the House!

This was a big headache in my business. I think you will find most daycare providers will say somewhat the same.

When caring for friends and family, stand your ground, although they don't have to be a friend or a relative to try for a freebie. My advice to this is don't do it.

I learned the hard way. Let me tell you a little story.

Once there was a lady, whom I will call Mooch Mama. Mooch Mama had three little children, two girls and a boy.

These children were so easy to care for they were good kids. I did daycare for six weeks for these three kids. Yes, I am nuts, and, yes, I said six (6) weeks. At that time, I charged $85.00 per week, per child, for full time. This is a total of $255.00 per week. So you figure $255.00 X 6 weeks = $1,530.00. That's not a small chunk of change, especially when you are feeding, bathing, and keeping the children over night, because Mooch Mama never learned how to tell time.

When I provided care for children, I accepted payments from the state. There are many state programs (in Michigan and possible other states as well) that help working parents' pay for childcare services. Each person who receives state help receives different amounts and types of help.

It goes like this; Parents calls provider, ask for services and if provider accept state payments. Provider either says yes or no, then sets up an interview, if yes. Parent comes to interview, provider accepts kids and parent as client. Parent at the time of interview presents state papers for provider to fill out. Provider fills out papers, hands them back to parent, who is suppose to turn them into their state case worker. Then, after receiving the papers from the parents, the state, usually sends the provider a letter showing the amount the state will pay. At that point the provider usually receives a check in about four to six weeks, after care has been provided.

Now, usually, most parents that receive state help are trying hard to better themselves. Consequently, they, *DO*, turn in their state forms to their caseworker, hence so the provider can be paid for services, already rendered. Just for the record, this is the parents' responsibility to turn in the papers to their caseworkers.

Anyways, I believed the mother when she told me she had turned in the papers for help from the state. Well, after waiting and watching, nothing, came in the mailbox. So, I called the state office and asked her caseworker. Sometimes the state was late with payments. Mooch Momma's caseworker didn't even know she was working. Therefore, Mooch Momma had never turned in any papers for childcare. She was employed at a local bar, receiving state money and working as well, but her caseworker didn't even know. Hum, go figure.

I confronted Mooch Mama, who told me this demoralizing story about how her boy friend beat her up, hit the children, and how they loved me so much because I took such good care of them. "Please don't kick my children out. It's not their fault," she exclaimed.

I told her I would accept $900.00. If she could get the payment to me, I would call it even. Big mistake. First, never-never let someone go that far into debt with you. Second, never-never-bargain your money with anyone.

To make a very long story short, I took her to small claims court and sued her. Yes, I won but it was up to me to collect. When I filed to sue her, at that time in Michigan the cost was $32.00, plus an extra $25.00 to have the papers delivered by an officer of the law. I took all my papers to court and had everything looking good and professional. I told my story, and she told hers, and the magistrate felt sorry for Mooch Mama, and lowered the charges to $600.00 (instead of the $1,530.00 which is what I wanted, since she could not work with me on the $900.00 agreement I asked for earlier). Mooch Mama laid this sob story on the magistrate about how she was single, on welfare, car broke down, couldn't get to work-you name it she bellowed it. Yes, I said how unfair that was, since I was a single mother myself and was paying my way through college at that time, and had two boys to support. It did no good. That was many years ago, and I have received one $50.00 payment from her, two days after court. That did not even cover the court costs. So here is a lesson that I hope you learn never let debts go. Collect as soon as you can, remember this your paycheck!

Tribulations With Parents

One time I had a parent who insisted that I not give her daughter a nap with the rest of the children. Why, I asked. The parent told me that when the daughter napped at my house, she would not go to sleep for her until 8:30, and she needed her time, too. I found that a little weird, and I would not comply with her nap theory. Of course, she screamed at me and said she was turning me in for not listening to her request. I had to chuckle at that one. I told her to feel free to call as many people as she felt she needed.

I guess the reason I laughed at that was the fact that she dropped the girl off at 2:00 p.m. and didn't pick her up until 8:00 p.m., and she had to drive 20 minutes to get home from the daycare. So I guess for her to want to rush straight home and put her daughter to bed was a little weird to me. Who am I though? She obviously needed her time, too.

Another time, I had a parent with three children, one of whom was a baby. The baby was 6 weeks old when I took him, and the mother told me that, since I was on the food program for the older children and they didn't eat that much, I could cut her some slack in payments for the baby. She felt that I was making too

66

much money and even told me so. She told me that, "babysitters" were not supposed to be rich. I had to laugh at, that because at that time I lived in a town house, drove a tin can for a car, and was living from check to check. Nevertheless, I was rich, ha ha ha.

The outcome of that situation was termination, because the mother could not understand why I wanted to charge her for all three of her children. I gave her a second child discount, and when her third was born, we sat down together and worked out a payment that was suitable for both her and I. However, a few weeks went by, and she felt she paid too much. The funny thing was the state paid all but $13.00 per week for all three children. She felt that was too much for 45 hours per week and three kids. Yea, right! I guess that's how it goes sometimes.

Some parents feel that, as a provider you should teach their children everything they need to know and the way the parents tell us to do. You know, let them run our business for us. What a wonderful idea, and why don't you come and clean up after all the kids, cook for them, color with them, and do all the things that I do, while you're at it. Then, maybe, you can tell me how to run my business.

Tribulations With Children

As a provider, you are going to experience so many things. You will cry and laugh, sometimes at the same time. Most of the children I have cared for were actually great, and not many had problems. Yet when they do have a problem, it becomes your problem too. This is where you must learn to deal with situations as they arise.

I found that a lot of children cry, or have outburst's of a mean streak, or tell you "NO, I DON"T HAVE TO." Well, let's face it; they are being put in a new home with a lot of strange people. Then, there is the mean old provider. Provider who actually becomes their friend in due time, that is. For most of the problems with children, you will find that talking it out works very well. But sometimes the problem can go deeper than the surface of their little faces. That is where you will really need to study the situation and decide what you are going to do. You always have to explain things to parents when such problems occur. Yet not all parents are willing to listen to what you, as a provider, have to say. This is when you will have to make the choice of, is this a bad thing or a not-so-bad thing? Sometimes these choices are touchy on the provider's part.

Unbelievable Questions From Parents

I bet you are thinking, what does she mean? Well, if you don't know yet, you will. It won't take long. These are requests that will stand the hair up on your neck and keep it there for a few days. Usually something that makes you laugh when you go to sleep at night, and even for the next few days.

One time I had a single dad. I provided care for his 4-year-old daughter. The child was sweet, but a pill to wake up. Dad would drop her off at 10:00 p.m. and pick her up at 7:00 a.m. throughout the week. I was having a tough time getting her up, so I thought I would let her sleep until Dad came, thinking, because it's so early, he could carry her to the car. Dad gets here to pick her up, and I told him she must have had a full day yesterday, because she seemed tired and I couldn't get her up. Dad asked me if I thought it would be *ok* to give her coffee to keep her awake. I told him that was something I would never do personally, but to ask his doctor why she was so tired.

This is the funny part, it turned out the kid was so tired because all through the week Dad picked her up at 7:00 a.m. then, she had no nap all day, and she never went to sleep until about 10:30 p.m. I guess that might even make me tired.

Another brainless moment was when a parent asked to see my bedroom. I told them no, because I didn't use my bedroom for daycare. The parent insisted on seeing what I had to hide (possible, bra or panties on the floor and I didn't make my bed daily either). I told him, "I have nothing to hide, but you are not going into my personal bedroom." He then told me I had to let him in there, and if I didn't, he would turn me into the license beaureau. I told him to feel free to tell anyone he liked, then proceeded to let him know that his behavior was not acceptable to me and he would have to find services elsewhere. About that time he laughed and said, "Oh, I'm only kidding with you," I laughed as well and told him, "I not." Behavior like this is just not acceptable to me, and I hope you never accept it, either.

I interviewed a lady who wanted to use my services, until, I told her that her daughter would have to lie down at nap time, which was at 9:30 p.m. (I did second shift).

The lady told me that I had to keep her daughter up, because she was hiring me to work for her, I was not doing the hiring. Yea, sure. That interview was over quickly.

I once had a parent ask if I would bring their child home and pick them up. They offered to pay an additional $1.00 per day for my gas and trouble. I should have done that, an extra five $5.00 per week. Just think of all the stuff I could have purchased with that. Did they even think about the insurance liability, about the trouble loading up all the other children, dragging them in and out every day for a five-minute ride around the corner? That's what really got to me, they lived around the corner from me. Some parents expect too much!

Another parent asked if I could cook extra for her and her husband. She told me that she got home too late to cook dinner, and it was too much on her to do that entire wife stuff. I told her, "I am not your maid," then told her about frozen dinners.

In the years I have did daycare for children I can say that I had a lot of brainless requests from parents. Some will stick with you until you die, and others will vanish quickly. Overall, there are some real good stories to tell.

Protective Services

This is a nightmare that a provider would like to avoid. Nevertheless, it is a subject that should be mentioned. As a provider, it is your responsibility to provide care for, and to protect the children. Protect them while they are in your care. You ask, protect them from what? Parents, brothers, sisters, aunts, uncles, etc. Sexual molesters, child beaters, verbal and mental abusers. They are out there, and with any luck they will all get caught. Unfortunately, many of these monsters will get away with the abuse that they perpetrate.

I would like to share with you an incident that happened to me. Within my first little bit of doing day-care, I was caring for a baby (I will call this child Baby Doe). This baby was approximately six months old. I cared for Baby Doe approximately 10 hours a day, five days a week. Baby Doe was a wonderful baby.

The first thing was the phone call. The mother told me she had seen my ad at the laundramat. I thought, this is wonderful, my ad is being noticed, and I'm getting phone calls. This is what it's all about.

The mother sounded great on the phone. We talked about 30 minutes, and I set up an interview for the next day. The next day came, and it was great. Mom was wonderful. I thought that you could not have asked for a better mommy. She seemed to love her baby very much. Baby Doe looked very clean, well fed, and healthy. I was more than happy to sign on with this woman and accept her child into my home.

The first week of childcare was great, as well. Mom would drop Baby Doe off early in the morning and pick him up late in the evening. I noticed nothing at all wrong the first week. Everything seemed normal to me. Mom would kiss and love on Baby Doe like crazy. I never suspected anything. I don't think anybody would have suspected anything. Had you seen the way she was with her child.

The second week was a different story, a story that I wish would never have happened. Unfortunately, it did, and I witnessed it.

Mom started dropping off Baby Doe 15 to 20 minutes before her appointed time. I let this slide because I needed the money. Not only was Mom dropping

69

off Baby Doe earlier, but he was wet, hungry and dirty. His diaper was so soaked with urine it felt as if it weighed 20 pounds.

Baby Doe did not go back to sleep, which during the first week he had always done for about an hour. It took me about 20 minutes to get Baby Doe to calm down after being dropped off. He had on the very same clothes in which he had left my house the night before. The clothes smelt so strongly of urine, and they were so soiled, that I actually had to take them off Baby Doe as soon as the mother left.

I gave Baby Doe a bath, fresh clothes, a clean diaper and food every morning for the second week. Taking care of Baby Doe did not bother me. However, the fact was, that Baby Doe was coming to my house every morning in this fashion. He also seemed different. I could not put my finger on why Doe seemed different; I just knew that he was. He would relax in my arms every morning after I did the over-haul. I would sit in my rocker, put a little blanket over Baby Doe, and rock and sing him to sleep. It was such a great feeling to cuddle an infant; they are so precious and innocent.

During this second week, when mother dropped off the baby, as well as picked him up, I noticed her attitude had changed. She was very quick and loud, not like she had been before. She seemed to be nervous and unsettled.

Once during this week, when Mom was picking up, Baby Doe started crying when she walked in the door. Mom walked over, grabbed Baby Doe out of the playpen, held him up into the air, shook him then, told Baby Doe to "Shut the hell up!"

I was dumbfounded. I told mother, "This will not happen in my home. You cannot talk to Doe like that here, and you should not talk to him like that at any time. Baby is just that, a baby."

Mom looked at me, shook her head, and said, "Oh yea, I know. I don't usually do that. I just had a hard day." I didn't say anything to her after she said that. I just looked at her as she took Doe and left my home.

The next day there was another incident. This time Baby Doe was on the floor playing with blocks, laughing, and cooing. Mom walked in. Doe looked up, saw her and started crying. I thought to myself, this is crazy, Baby Doe is supposed to be happy to see Mom. Doe shook as I had never seen a baby shake before. This scared me.

Mom walked over to Baby Doe, grabbed Baby's little jacket and started putting it on him. Any baby will fight you when you change their diapers and dress them, and Doe did as well. Mom grabbed his arm and shoved it in the arm sleeve. While doing this, she caught baby's finger, and it was bending backwards. I noticed and said, "Oh no-stop! You caught baby's little finger. That must be why baby is crying."

Mom looked at me and said, "Oh, well. Then baby will have to learn to be tough, huh?"

She didn't stop. She kept shoving baby's arm through. I said, "That's mean. I can't believe you are doing that!"

I was so upset at this point. I just wanted to tell her to leave without Baby Doe. I knew at this point what I had to do. I didn't like it, but I could see things were getting rough with her and her baby.

The next day was *ok*. It was the day after that made me almost make a dreadful phone call to Child Protective Services. This was at the end of the second week. Mom came to get baby, and the usual happened again. Mom walked in and baby started crying. This time she picked up Baby Doe and threw him on my couch. Yes, you read this correctly-I said, threw baby. Before I could get out a word, she grabbed him off the couch, slammed him onto the floor, and pushed his face into the floor very hard. So hard that he got a bloody nose. I was furious at this point, she immediately jumped up and ran out the door, yelling, "I will see and pay you next week."

I called my friend who was another daycare provider and told her everything that had happened. I told her that, "I'm calling Protective Services and report the mother." I just needed to calm down, so I could talk clearly to them.

Much to my surprise, as I was talking to my friend, there was a beep. I had call waiting. It was the Child Protective Services. I was amazed and relieved.

I spoke with a man whom I will call Mr. Cool. He was really nice and very understanding of the situation. He started asking me questions about Baby Doe's mother. I asked him how he knew this was going on, I hadn't even made the call to him yet. He kind of laughed and told me that there were two other calls about this woman, and that he was doing his homework.

To make the rest of this very long story a little shorter, Mr. Cool and a woman whom I will call Mrs. Nice made an appointment and came to my home to visit while Baby Doe was in my care. I was more than happy to talk face to face to them. I told them about the incidents that had happened at my home. I told them everything-the way the interview went, and how sweet Baby Doe's mother had been at first, then how she had turned into a different person after just one week.

Baby Doe was taken out of his mothers' custody later that day. Dad was given temporary custody of Baby Doe. I was subpoenaed to court and had to testify in Baby Doe's behalf. The outcome was that Mom admitted to most of the abuse, and acted as if it was no big deal. Two other people testified in Baby Doe's behalf, as well. They seen her actually slap Baby Doe in the face, yell and scream at baby during the night, and refuse to feed him because she felt he was too fat.

I was sick to my stomach after I heard everything that others had seen. I am sure these people were telling the truth-Mom admitted to it. She told the judge, "This is the way I was brought up, and this is the way I will bring up my child, and no one will stop me." Well, stop her they did, and it's a good thing. Dad and his new wife have full custody of the child and I have seen him once since the incident. He seems very happy, healthy and not abused.

You never know if something like this will happen to you, but if it does please don't hesitate to call and report it. You owe this to the children and to yourself. Baby Doe went through a terrible experience, and I felt so sorry for him. I was relieved to see him put into in a much more stable and refreshing atmosphere, and to have the loving parents he deserved.

Child Abuse

Child abuse can consists of many different types of abuse that jeopardizes or harms a child's physical or emotional health and development. I have put together a small list to help aid you in becoming aware of the different types of abuse.

Types of Abuse

Physical abuse - Non-accidental like, hitting, kicking, shaking, burning, biting, choking and throwing.

Emotional abuse - Mental health and social development like, yelling, screaming, calling names and shaming.

Sexual abuse - Sex acts between an adult and a child, meaning fondling, intercourse, pornography and child prostitution.

Neglect - physical - Failure to providing for physical needs such as, carelessness of supervision, unsuitable housing, lack of food and clothing, abandonment, denial of medical care, and unsatisfactory hygiene.

Neglect- emotional - Failure to give affection for development of a child such as, emotional, social, physical, ignoring, not exchange a few words, like, "I love you," lack of credit and positive reinforcement.

If you suspect abuse, please don't hesitate call the National Child Abuse Hotline number, it's toll free. You can call anonymously.

The National Child Abuse Hotline number is 1-800-4-A-CHILD.

10

A DAY IN THE LIFE OF A PROVIDER

Daily Routines

Make a plan and run with it. I lived by my daily plan. Things went very well, and the children loved it. I would try to plan meals, projects and playtime. Here is a copy of the daily routine I used with my daycare. You can make your own. Set your own times for when and what you wish to do.

Peg's Copy of Things I Did

- ✓ Finger plays: (last about 20-30 minutes) we turn out the lights, take a flashlight and shine it on the wall, and make finger-play shadows.
- ✓ Song and dance time: (30 minutes) everyone sings and dances.
- ✓ Project time: (30 minutes) everyone gets to make something. We would make special projects for holidays.
- ✓ Movie time: (This started at 9:30 p.m.–11:00 p.m. close) everyone watches a movie, during quiet time.
- ✓ Story time: (15-30 minutes, depends on story) everyone listens to a story.
- ✓ Free play times: (whenever) everyone can play with toys of choice.
- ✓ Pick-up time: (whenever) everyone picks up all the toys.
- ✓ Outside time: (whenever) depends on the weather.
- ✓ Nature walks: (whenever) we all go around and look for different nature stuff, and talk and gather some, too.
- ✓ Picnics: (Friday's dinner time-5:00) If weather permits, we have a picnic in the yard or park.

Sometimes when we had a picnic planned, it would rain, so we compromised. I would get an old blanket, spread it out in the toy room, and we would have our picnic right there.

We would all pretend we were outside and some of the children would make different sounds such as a tiger, lion, dog, cat or birds. This is a very fun thing to do with children, and sometimes I actually hoped it would rain, just to listen to their little imaginations go wild. We would also have a special story. Sometimes the children made up their own stories, which was a real treat.

Songs and Stuff

Peggy wore an old dress (use old shirt for boys)
An old dress
An old dress
Peggy wore an old dress all day long.
(Insert each child's name in the song)

Yum, yum, yum!
Yum, yum, yum!
That's the way that (what ever you are eating) tastes!
Yum, yum, yum!
(Good picnic song)

Peg's "Banana Song"

Peg Sings:

I'm a little monkey in my tree, eating all the bananas I can see.

Kids Sing:

Hey, you monkey up in that tree! I am a little hungry, can't you see? Would you share a few of those bananas with me?

Peg Sings:

Well…maybe. Let's see

Everyone Sings:

One, two, three, four (keep counting up to 10/20/50/100, whatever you like).

I purchased some play bananas at my local store, and when we sang this song I would pass out a play banana to each child and keep going till all the bananas were passed out.

I made this up song all by myself, and the kids loved it. Me too!

A Bunch of Little Daycare Chit-a-lings:

(Sing to the tune of "Ten Little Indians")

One little, two little, three little chit-a-lings,
Four little, five little, six little chit-a-lings,
Seven little, eight little, nine little chit-a-lings, all in a row.

Things to do

What I weigh

Use your bathroom scale and weigh each child. Then have the kids draw a scale showing their weight. This teaches the children how to weigh themselves and the use of numbers with art.

My Foot

Draw around child's foot and let him/her color or paint it. Then they can try to guess whose foot is whose.

Look, It's Me!

Put a photo of each child in a box. Give them each a turn to pick out a picture and tell who it is. Then let that child tell his/her favorite color or food. Then it is that person turn to pick the next picture.

Cheesy Mice

Cut yellow paper in to the shapes of triangle cheese and draw a small mouse or stick a mouse sticker in the middle. Then tell a story about a mouse, or have cheese food for snacks.

Naptime Mice

To get ready for a nap, have the children pretend they are all mice and tell them to see who can be the quietest. Works for seeing who can be the fastest mouse, too, the first one to sleep (Sneaky old Mama Mouse).

Peg's Brown Bag Nature Find

1 brown lunch bag, 1 list of 10-15 things to find. Give the children a bag and a list, take them on a nature walk, and see if they can find what's on their list. You might want to make the list to fit the different ages you have. Some things I put on my list were:

You must find:

4 acorns
3 yellow leaves
1 small stick that looks like a letter
5 little rocks that are black and flat
2 red leaves
1 baby pinecone
Easy stuff they can find on the trail you walk.

Macaroni Necklaces

Colored noodles
String/yarn
String the noodles, and you have a necklace!

Rainy Day Stuff to Do

Edible Play Dough

½ cup brown sugar
½ cup peanut butter
1 tablespoon oatmeal

Mix and play, then eat, if you like.

Jello Doddle's

You will need saltshakers, pencils, craft glue and different colors of jello. Draw a picture on the paper, and then line it with glue. Sprinkle different colors of jello on the paper.

Peg's Ponderings

You can have fundraisers at your daycare, also. Contact people you know who sell different things and ask them about fundraisers. I did well with Tupperware. They have great items and seem to have many specials, and you can earn free items, as well. I have a friend who lives in Baltimore, Maryland, and he said, that pizza sales do well in his area. You can have juice sales, with cookies or different treats. This helps you get the things you, use a lot, such as: crayons, scissors, paper, markers, and glue. Have a Friday yard sale, ask parents if they can donate some items. You would be surprised at what parents like to toss out.

If you do well with the fundraisers, you can purchase a big item, such as: Fisher Price Gym Set, teeter-totter, or a sand box. Get the children to help you sell, the parents take it to work, and other relatives. It works. This is a good thing!

Supply List

Things you might want to purchase:

- ✓ Construction paper
- ✓ Cotton balls
- ✓ Crayons

- ✓ Glue
- ✓ Markers
- ✓ Paints
- ✓ Paper plates
- ✓ Scissors
- ✓ Buttons
- ✓ Counting games
- ✓ Magnets
- ✓ Magnifying glass
- ✓ Musical instruments
- ✓ Puzzles
- ✓ Blocks
- ✓ Lincoln Logs
- ✓ Chalk for outside and inside
- ✓ Balls
- ✓ Dolls/Barbie's/GI Joes
- ✓ Books

Burn Out

Ok, here you are, and everything is peachy keen. Everyone loves your daycare, and everyone loves you. What could make you burn out on your business? Who knows?

There have been way too many studies to mention here about why one gets spent in the daycare field, but the truth of the matter is, hey, we all get spent at times. What I would recommend to help avoid this spent situation is brain-err-cises. Yes, I know it's not really a word; but, heckey-darn, expand your mind in activities and things for your business.

I don't care how wonderful the children are, or the parents never pay late and never upset you. You might get to a point where you feel burn out. Here are a few suggestions I have for burn outs.

- ✓ Exercise daily.
- ✓ Eat right.
- ✓ Take time for yourself every day. Even if it's only 15 minutes, take the time.
- ✓ Don't take on extra tasks that you really don't wish to do.
- ✓ Every morning when you wake up, think, wow, I am alive and that's a good thing!
- ✓ Try to keep your stresses few and far between.

- ✓ Talk to people over three feet tall at night to help keep your mind in balance.
- ✓ Avoid extra paper work, if possible.
- ✓ Pace yourself, be strong.
- ✓ Last but certainly not my least, if you believe in Jesus, pray!

Guide in Preparing Your Home For Inspection

Policies and Plans

Is your certification posted?
Are you certified by the American Red Cross?
Are your emergency plans written and posted?

a) Serious accident/injuries
b) Fire evacuation
c) Tornado

Do you have a written discipline policy?
Do all assistants know the policy?
Have you given a copy to all parents?

Records

Do you have a complete Child Information Card on file for each child?
Do you have a completed Child in Care Statement on file for each family?
Do you have medication slips for each child?

Your Toys and Equipment

Do you have an adequate supply of, and variety of, both toys and equipment?
Are your toys and equipment safe and clean?
Do you have cribs or playpens for the children less than 12 months old to sleep in?
Do you have a comfortable, safe, clean place for the other children to rest?
If you use the floor, is it padded, warm and free from drafts?

Household

Remove all hazardous items from:

a) Under your kitchen sink
b) Under your bathroom sink
c) All medicine cupboards

Make sure that the following is out of the reach of children:

Children

a) All cleaning and laundry supplies.
b) Plastic bags of any type.
c) All sharp objects (scissors, knives).
d) Matches, lighters, etc.
e) Medicines of any kind.
f) Make-up, perfumes, shampoos, etc.
g) Super glue, alcohol, bug sprays, and kerosene.
h) Poisonous plants.
i) Are all guns locked up and out of the reach of children?
j) Do you have your ammunition in a different place from where you keep your guns?

Everything that is flammable moves four feet away from your furnace. Fireplace owners make sure your hearth is padded. Make sure all your heat-producing equipment is shielded to prevent burns (furnace, water heater, wood-burning stoves, fireplaces, registers, pipes). Make sure your smoke detectors are working, and that you have one on each floor.

Check with your local Department of Social Services and see what type of fire extinguisher you need, then mount one on each floor. Make sure your electrical outlets are covered.

Make sure all your doorway gates and stairways are protected. Make sure your handrails and banisters are solid and on decks and stairways. Make sure everyone knows that smoking is not permitted on the premises during your business hours.

Diapering Space

Do you have a specific area where you change babies? If so, make sure it's clean and not by your eating area, Yuk.

Your Pets

Make sure all your pets are up to date on their shots. Give your pets a place to get away from the children. Some pets might not tolerate having their eyes poked, ears pulled, being hit and many more torturous animal kid abuse some children might inflict. Your pets, might retaliate, and, bite. Keep their food away from the children, as well. If you have a cat make sure, you keep the litter box away from the children. Some things don't always taste as good as they look.

Your Outside Play Area

Check your yard for hazardous things such as nails, broken glass, poisons. Is your yard fenced in? Should you be next to a busy road, you might want to consider this.

If you have a sand box, make sure no four-legged creatures use it for a potty. If you have outside pets, make sure your play area and the pets' areas are separate. Keep your yard clean of animal feces.

Water Hazards

If you are close to, or have, a pool, pond, river or any other kind of water hazard, check with your local Department of Social Services to find out what your guidelines are for distance from your home, as well as any other kind of precautions necessary to prevent drowning.

Using Your Basement

I would recommend that you call your local Department of Social Services and find out what the rules and regulations are on basements in your state.

Behavior Methods

Give consistent love and attention to all children equally. Always supervise. Make sure you understand that children watch you, and when you display your angry reactions to a problem, you are teaching them it's *ok* to act this way. Teach the children how to solve their problems with peace and respect for others. Never spank, hit or raise your voice. Don't let the children sit and watch TV all day-limit it.

Peg's Final Ponder

I can't tell you the secret to staying in the business for 25 years or even 15 years. What I can tell you is to remind yourself why you are doing this business, and what it is about the business that you like. Tell yourself often; actually sit down and write it out. It works. Don't avoid your problems; nip them in the bud at the beginning and you will sleep better at night. Don't let others run your business. This is your home and your business. You don't have to accept anyone you don't want. The reason I enjoyed my business so much was the enjoyment I got from the success of the children. I would teach them something, and the next day the parent would tell me how neat it was.

My business was fulfilling, hard work even smelly at times-but fun. I enjoyed my daycare immensely. I would not give up those memories for anything. I am glad I took the chance and opened up.

Not only did I make a lot of new friends and get into the public eye, I supported my two children and myself with ease. We took many weekend vacations. We went out of state on vacations for two weeks at a time. I treated myself to a vacation in Las Vegas.

I am not saying that you are going to get rich, but I am telling you that if you budget your money and watch your spending, you can have nice things, not just vacations. The first year, I had to work one other job along with the daycare. I really don't know what I would have done without my oldest son, Anthony, to help me in the beginning. My youngest son, J.P. helped with many things in the business as he became a little older.

My second year was a little better. I didn't make too much more, but we did better. Don't forget, I was a single mom, and some of you will do much better than I did. I closed my daycare to begin a writing career, and I hope this is a good start. I also write children's and adult books. I hope you use this book as a guide, I hope it helps you in your business. God bless, and I hope you prosper!

Appendixes

Appendix A Current State Licensing offices
Appendix B Child Nutritional Programs
Appendix C Child Care Organizations and helpful web sites

Public Information Numbers

Alabama
Department of Human Resources
(334) 242-1850

Alaska
Department of Health & Social Services
(907) 269-7801

Arizona
Department of Economic Security
(602) 5432-5210

Arkansas
Department of Human Services
(501) 682-8650

California
California Health and Human Services Agency
(916) 657-2268

Colorado
Department of Human Services
(303) 866-5822

Connecticut
Department of Children and Families
(860) 550-6305

Delaware
Department of Health and Social Services
(302) 577-4501

District of Columbia
D.C. Department of Human Services
(202) 279-6113

Florida
Department of Children and Families
(850) 488-4855

Georgia
Georgia DHR – Division of Family and Children Services
(404) 651-8409

Hawaii
Department of Human Services
(808) 586-4888

Idaho
Department of Human Services
(208) 334-5500

Illinois
Department of Human Services
(217) 557-1651

Indiana
Family and Social Services Administration
(317) 232-4490

Iowa
Department of Human Services
(515) 281-4847

Kansas
Department of Social Services and Rehabilitation Services
(785) 296-4684

Kentucky
Kentucky CFS Department for Community Based Services
(502) 564-3703

Louisiana
Department of Social Services

(225) 342-6729

Maine
Department of Human Services
(207) 287-2546

Maryland
Department of Human Resources
(410) 767-7758

Massachusetts
Department of Social Services
(617) 748-2000

Michigan
Family Independence Agency
(517) 373-7394

Minnesota
Department of Human Services
(651) 296-4416

Mississippi
Department of Human Services
(601) 359-4480

Missouri
Department of Social Services
(573) 751-4815

Montana
Division of Human and Community Services
(406) 444-1788

Nebraska
Health and Human Services System
(402) 471-9108

Nevada
Department of Human Resources
(775) 687-4832

New Hampshire
Division for Children and Families
(603) 271-4837

New Jersey
Department of Human Services
(609) 292-3703

New York
Office of Children and Families Services
(518) 473-7793

North Carolina
Department of Health and Human Services
(919) 733-9190

North Dakota
Department of Human Services
(701) 328-4933

Ohio
Department of Human Services
(614) 466-6650

Oklahoma
Department of Human Services
(405) 521-3027

Oregon
Department of Human Resources
(503) 945-5738

Pennsylvania
Department of Public welfare
(717) 787-4592

Rhode Island
Department of Human Services
(401) 528-3575

South Carolina
Department of Social Services
(803) 898-7602

South Dakota
Department of Social Services
(605) 773-3165

Tennessee
Department of Children's Services
(615) 741-9192

Texas
Department of Human Services
(512) 438-3045

Utah
Department of Human Services
(801) 538-3991

Vermont
Agency of Human Services
(802) 241-2226

Virginia
Department of Social Services
(804) 692-1031

Washington
Department of Social and Health Services
(360) 902-7828

West Virginia
Bureau for Children and Families
(304) 558-0999

Wisconsin
Department of Health and family Services
(608) 266-1683

Wyoming
Department of Family Services
(307) 777-7564

Appendix B

Public numbers for Child Nutritional Programs.

Alabama
334-242-1988

Alaska
907-465-8708

Arizona
602-542-8709

Arkansas
501-324-9502

California
916-323-7311
1-800-952-5609

Colorado
303-866-6661

Connecticut
860-807-2070

Delaware
302-739-4676

District Of Columbia
202-576-7400

Florida
850-245-4323

Georgia
404-562-7099

Guam
671-475-6407

Hawaii
808-733-8400

Idaho
208-332-6820

Illinois
217-782-2491

Indiana
317-232-0850

Iowa
515-281-4757

Kansas
785-296-2276

Kentucky
502-573-4390

Louisiana
225-342-3720

Maine
207-287-5060

Maryland
410-767-0199

Massachusetts
781-338-6479

Michigan
517-373-8642

Minnesota
651-582-8526

Mississippi
601-354-7015

Missouri
573-751-6251
1-800-733-6251

Montana
406-444-1828
1-888-307-9333

Nebraska
402-471-3566

Nevada
775-687-9154

New Hampshire
603-271-3860

New Jersey
609-984-0692

New Mexico
505-827-1821

New York
518-473-3921

North Carolina
919-715-1940

North Dakota
701-328-2294

Ohio
614-466-2945
1-800-808-MEAL

Oklahoma
405-521-3327

Oregon
503-378-3579 ext. 467

Pennsylvania
717-787-7698

Puerto Rico
787-754-0790

Rhode Island
401-222-4600 ext. 2364

South Carolina
803-734-9500

South Dakota
605-773-3413

Tennessee
615-313-4749

Texas
512-997-6550

Utah
801-538-7513

Vermont
802-828-5154

U.S. Virgin Islands
340-774-9373

Virginia
804-225-2074

Washington
360-753-3580

West Virginia
304-558-2708

Wisconsin
608-267-9121

Wyoming
307-777-7494

Appendix C

Child Care Organizations

The list I have gathered for you is just an extra list of some of the childcare programs that might be a good source. This list is not a full count of all resources and programs, you may ask the National Associations on information in the child care field in your area for more programs and organizations.

The Council for Professional Recognition
2460 16th NW
Washington DC 20009-3575
202-265-9090
Fax: 202-265-7309
www.cdacouncil.org

They specialize in credentialing/certification of care providers for infants and toddlers through kindergarten.

National Associate for the Education of Young Children
1509 Sixteenth Street NW
Washington, DC 20036
(800) 424-2460
www.naeyc.org

This is a group of childhood educators. They publish brochures, posters, videotapes and book. They offer training and network meetings and more.

Redleaf Press
450 North Syndicate Suite 5
Saint Paul, MN 55104-4125
(800) 423-8309

They'll provide you with a resource catalog, books and some publications for providers.

Funsteps, Inc.
5112 Hillsboro Avenue North
New Hope, MN 55442
800-882-7332
www.funsteps.com

Funsteps offers curriculum and teaching materials for working with young children. Their featured product is a complete package of activities that includes both the curriculum and the supplies. All curriculum products follow the Kapers for Kids curriculum program. Free information and samples are available.

Child Care Food Programs

US Department of Agriculture
Washington, DC 20250

The National Child Abuse Hotline
1-800-4-A-CHILD